Es Selendang Mayang

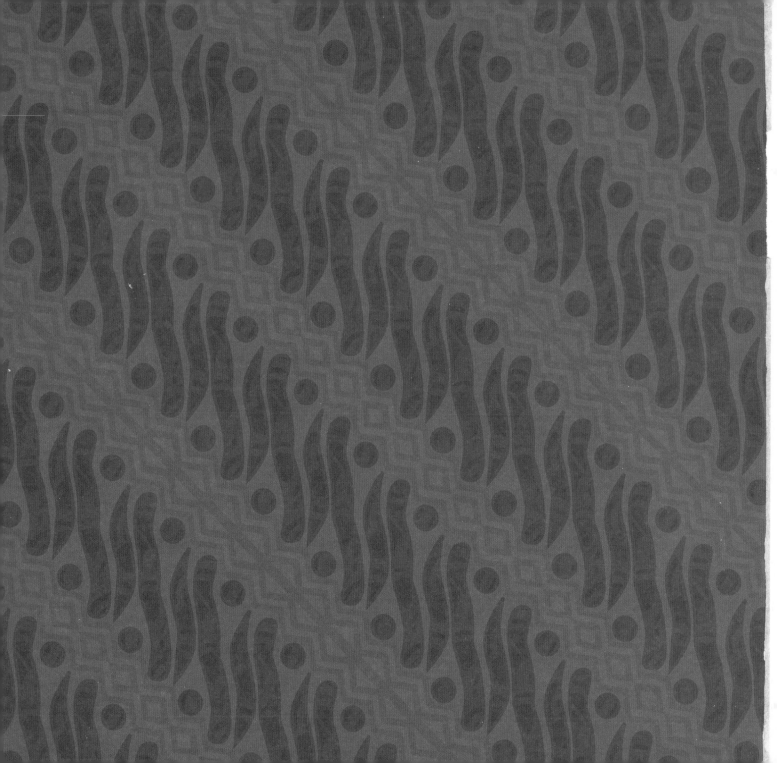

DINA YUEN

Indonesian Cooking

SATAYS, SAMBALS AND MORE

81 Homestyle Recipes with the True Taste of Indonesia

foreword by **Glenn Chu**
Indigo Restaurant, Hawaii

TUTTLE Publishing

Tokyo | Rutland, Vermont | Singapore

Traditional stone mortar and pestle

Coconut Noodle Soup

Fresh Springroll ingredients

Contents

Above **Indonesian Fried Chicken**
Left **Crispy Fish with Chili Sauce**

Crisp Tofu with Sweet Spicy Sauce

Spicy Lemongrass Beef

A Symphony of Surprising Flavors

In 1994, a few months before I opened my Honolulu restaurant, Indigo, my wife, Barbara and I traveled to Indonesia and Thailand on a serendipitous shopping and eating trip. Our plan was to find unique furnishings and architectural pieces that would create a sensual ambience for our diners. More than I expected, our travels turned out to be a revelation for my palate as well. This was my first trip to Asia—the first of many—and it greatly deepened my love affair with its glorious food. Barbara and I spent over a month traveling throughout the islands of Java and Bali. While hunting for treasures, we discovered the vibrant, multi-layered cuisine unique to this part of the world. From fiery hot sambals to spicy coconut-based curries, crisp banana fritters to creamy durian ice cream—each provided a symphony of delicious, often surprising flavors–many of which I later adapted into signature Indigo dishes.

Within these pages, a culinary adventure awaits you. With Chef Dina as your expert guide, you can explore the planet's largest archipelago—the fabled Spice Islands— and its distinctive cuisine in your own kitchen. Dina's clear, easy-to-follow recipes capture the spirit of Indonesian cooking—a diverse, little known cuisine she makes accessible to anyone. Ranging from the familiar, such as Chicken and Beef Satay, Fresh Spring Rolls (*Lumpia Basah*), Indonesian Mixed Salad with Creamy Peanut Dressing (*Gado Gado*) and Traditional Nasi Goreng, to the more exotic, such as Spicy Lemongrass Beef (*Daging Asam Pedas*), Carmelized Pork (*Babi Kecap*), Grilled Swordfish with Fragrant Yellow Rice (*Ikan Bakar dengan Nasi Kuning*), or Tamarind Roasted Shrimp (*Asem Udang Bakar*), this collection of tantalizing recipes is certain to delight.

Dina not only shares her many years of cooking knowledge but clearly communicates her love of family and passion for food as well. In our memories, food is deeply rooted to those places and people we love. *The Indonesian Cookbook* celebrates food, its enticing flavors, tastes, and aromas, and the important role it plays in keeping us connected to friends and family.

glenn Chu

Glenn Chu
Chef/Owner, Indigo, Honolulu

Salad a la Mama

Organizing ingredients for stir-frying

Spicy Sauteed Calamari Rings

My Great Love of Indonesian Cuisine

Ever since childhood, I have equated food with love. Nearly every memory I have of gatherings with family and friends involves being around food. What could possibly be more important in life than great food and great company? My love affair with Indonesian cuisine began long before I even realized that's what it was. Having been blessed with wonderful parents who were world travelers, I had the opportunity to live in and visit many countries. Indonesia was host to a good number of my childhood years, profoundly contributing to what would become my lifetime passion for cooking and feeding people.

Indonesia and I have a very special relationship; it is after all, the place where many of my childhood memories take place. During those formative years, my parents educated my sisters and me on the great importance of the art of travel and food. Naturally, this education included the ap-

preciation of Indonesian cuisine. As a child though, I didn't always realize how lucky I was to have certain experiences or to be in a certain place. It wasn't until years later that I finally grew up enough to fully comprehend the priceless gift my parents had bestowed upon my sisters and me.

Every momentous occasion in Indonesia, whether it is a birthday, house warming, or office opening is celebrated with a *Tumpeng*. *Tumpeng* is a spectacular all-in-one feast of turmeric seasoned rice shaped into a gargantuan mountain top, with an assortment of side dishes that can range from the simple and inexpensive (fried chicken and soybean cakes) to the complex and extravagant (grilled seafood, potato cakes and a dozen other yummies). *Tumpengan*, or the day of *Tumpeng*, is the one day when all boundaries of race, age, class and any other distinctions are put aside to feast together, give thanks and pray

Tamarind Roasted Shrimp

Left **Savory Cucumber Relish**
Above **Oxtail Soup**

Sweet and Spicy Shredded Chicken

together, celebrate together. An Indonesian superstition dictates that whoever manages to eat the very tip of the rice will enjoy good luck for years to come. I never did have a chance to eat the proverbial mountaintop at any *Tumpengan* but I can safely say that good luck allowed me to partake in many of those glorious feasts.

I have been very fortunate to have had the opportunity to travel the 17,000 islands of Indonesia, though I've yet to set foot on each and every one of them. From east to west, north to south, the world's fourth most populous nation has an astoundingly vast array of indigenous cuisines to boast of, each as uniquely individual as its people and dialects. *Masakan Jawa*, for example, is the cuisine of eastern Java, predominantly the Surabaya area, famous for spicy salads and rich flavors. The fantasy island of Bali with all its lush greenery and untouched beaches, boasts a beautiful blend of sweet and mildly spicy roasted meats, showcasing the traditional methods of cooking in nature. Western Java offers two distinctly different cuisines, Betawi and Sunda, each with accents portraying Indonesia's long cultural and political history.

Along with my parents and siblings, I became a seasoned traveler and eater, going from the finest, world class dining establishments in five diamond hotels such as Ritz Carlton, Four Seasons, Aman Resorts and Mandarin Oriental to frequenting hole-in-the-wall restaurants only locals have known for decades. I ate Indonesian *Rijstaffel* in its finest presentations on delicate China with linen tablecloths and I ate *Es Campur* and *Bakmi Baso* on the streets of Jakarta and Surabaya, (the latter experiences when my mother was not around as she would be terrified of my contracting some dreadful malady from dirty water). The duality of such opposites became an addictive drug to me, each experience offering its unique set of flavors, scents, sounds, and emotions.

In my later teenage years, I experienced many of the most painful and trying moments of my life, losing my beloved grandfather and several other treasured family members. Those devastating losses shaped the course of my spirit and life irrevocably, often manifesting in the strangest of ways. In the kitchen, I began an insatiable quest for acute flavors, emotionally familiar aromas,

Traditional Coconut Rice Platter

A modern Indonesian feast

Tamarind Vegetable Soup

recreating recipes that were the favorites of people I'd lost forever. Aside from photo albums that were sometimes too difficult to look at, the recipes were all I had left to feel their embrace, to hear their laughter and the happy noises of loved ones eating together. From those early years until today, food has become the only viable bridge between those living in the present and those who have passed on.

Every time I miss my grandfather (or my uncles, aunts and cousins) I begin to cook his favorite dishes, many of which were Indonesian. From classic Indonesian Mapo Tofu (Mun Tahu) to Chicken Rice Porridge (Bubur Ayam), I often spend hours in the kitchen, creating one dish after another, as a silent offering to someone I love, who happens to be a little far away. I chop garlic at lightning speed, laughing to myself as I hear their voices, "*add more garlic…you can never have too much garlic.*" On my hands and knees, I maneuver the stone mortar and pestle to grind the red chili peppers, watching the ghost of my aunt showing me exactly how to bend my arm to get the right pressure. And when I'm done cooking, when I'm

done trying to make each dish a little better every time, I sit down with those loved ones around me today, sharing a wonderful home cooked meal. I give thanks for this new happy moment. For just a second, I close my eyes, I smell, I taste, and I am there again with the people who live in that most treasured place in my memory.

People who are unfamiliar with Indonesian cuisine always ask me "what is it like?" and I can only vaguely describe it as somewhere between Thai and Indian cuisine. It shares Thai cuisine's penchant for the intensely spicy and salty, and India's passion for rich curries. Really though, Indonesian food has its own unique range of flavors, ingredients, and techniques. Indonesian cuisine's unabashed use of fresh herbs and spices (such as garlic, turmeric, shrimp paste, Kaffir lime leaves and galangal) contribute to dishes that are fragrant and flavorful.

To have a complete grasp of Indonesian cuisine, it's imperative to understand that, from west to east, there are dramatically differing ingredients and techniques used in preparing meats, seafood, and vegetables. They stem from

Curried Chicken

Beef Satays

Stir-fried Noodles with Shrimp

Fresh chili peppers, garlic, and cilantro

cultural history and traditions that existed long before modern day restaurants and fancy kitchens.

The beautiful island of Bali is famous for its fresh seafood, which is no surprise considering the local abundance. But Bali differs from the rest of the nation in its culinary treatment of fresh seafood and meats. The ever popular *Bumbu Bali* refers to any seafood or meat that is first marinated in a rich coating of sweet soy sauce and a garlicky thick, red chili paste before grilling on an open air flame. What results is a succulent, sweet, and savory grilled meat or seafood dish with just a hint of spiciness.

Moving slightly west to the east coast of the main island of Java, is the metropolitan city of Surabaya and its surrounding neighbors, such as Malang. This eastern region is famous for its incredible desserts, including: old fashioned mocha cakes whipped up by grandmas in batik sarongs using butter; sweet and fluffy breads that make you forget all about calorie counting and the kind of ice cream cakes I had as a child that make me now desperately wish I could turn back the hands of time.

On the west coast in the capital city of Jakarta and its neighbors, we find yet another kind of indigenous Indonesian cuisine—rich curries simmering in old cauldrons, spicy fruit salads made with stone mortar and pestles and dishes that reflect the influences of foreign migrations into Indonesia in centuries past.

It's the commitment to using fresh ingredients, organic ingredients before the word organic became a fancy marketing gimmick; it's the fearless and bold use of herbs and spices and the relentless clinging to traditional methods that all come together to shape this spectacular country's unique and exotic foods.

Happy Cooking

Dina Yuen

A Few Tips and Techniques

The best way to ensure success in creating delicious Indonesian cuisine is getting organized and staying that way. Many of the tools and ingredients necessary in an Indonesian kitchen are now widely available in all Asian grocery stores and even in many Western markets. It's always a good idea to start off by investing the appropriate amount of time, effort, and money to purchase good quality ingredients and tools so that you don't end up wasting time or money.

Using a Mortar and Pestle Though we have modern day conveniences, such as food processors and blenders, there is nothing quite like using traditional tools. Out of all the mortar and pestles in existence, the Indonesian stone version is my absolute favorite. While using this tool does require a little physical exertion, the unique textures and flavors that result are well worth the effort. Make sure that the surface of the mortar is dry before placing the ingredients on it. When working with garlic or fresh chili peppers, a helpful trick is to sprinkle a little salt and/or sugar on top before mashing. The salt and sugar act as an abrasive helping to break everything down. Never pound the pestle in an up and down motion like you would with a meat pounder because of splattering. The Indonesian pestle has a curved structure, designed for angled and long strokes. Be firm with each stroke of the pestle against the mortar, almost as if you're dragging the ingredients along while firmly pushing down. You should also use a spoon to scrape the ingredients into the middle every so often so that you don't end up with a mess around the perimeter of the mortar. When finished, simply rinse the mortar and pestle under warm water and allow to air dry.

Using Fresh Ingredients I think it's important to use fresh ingredients whenever possible. In modern times, it can be tempting to purchase what appears to be easier alternatives in the form of canned, jarred, or frozen goods, but authentic Indonesian cuisine demands fresh ingredients to produce its array of complex flavors and textures. There are, however, certain preserved ingredients that are acceptable as substitutes for particular recipes without seriously compromising the integrity or quality of the dish. Ingredients such as coconut milk and palm sugar (*gula jawa*) are easily found in Asian markets in canned or packaged forms.

Working with Coconut Milk Coconut milk has a much lower burning temperature than many other liquids. When cooking with this rich liquid, remember to keep a close watch on it so it doesn't burn or boil over in the pot. Whether you're cooking a curry or a stew, it's important to stir often to avoid any ingredients sticking to the bottom of the pot or wok. If you use coconut milk to cook rice in a rice cooker, make sure to mix the rice gently with a wooden or plastic spatula even after the rice cooker says it's done cooking. After mixing the rice, allow it to sit on the cooker's warm setting for at least another 10 to 15 minutes before serving.

Working with Turmeric Turmeric is one of Indonesian cuisine's major ingredients, both in its fresh root and powdered forms. It can be difficult to find fresh turmeric in Western countries so I've substituted the powder form in these recipes. Similar to working with coconut milk and rice, when using turmeric in rice, you must mix the rice gently to spread the color and flavor of the turmeric evenly before and after the rice has cooked.

Stir-frying The most effective technique for ensuring great stir-fry dishes is to work with a large wok and wooden spatula. Gas stoves provide the optimum cooking situation because the heat will remain consistent, allowing you to stir-fry the ingredients quickly without burning. When stir-frying, always move the ingredients around with the spatula often and quickly. If you're working with an electric stove, you'll have to compensate for the lack of consistent heat by allowing the ingredients to remain at rest for longer periods of time between the actual stir-frying.

Stir-frying Rice or Noodles Working with large quantities of rice or noodles is no easy task. Without proper technique, you may end up with mushy rice and noodles that will fall apart. Borrowing from the general rules of stir-frying, start with a large wok and wooden spatula. The key to successful stir-fried rice and noodle dishes is to not mash these ingredients while cooking, but rather use the spatula to fold them over. Use your entire arm and elbow movement as opposed to a wrist action when stir-frying heavy ingredients. Don't

be afraid of scraping the wooden spatula all the way down into the bottom of the wok to ensure that no parts of the ingredients are left to burn while other parts are sitting uncooked on top. If you use your entire arm power rather than wrist movements, it will yield the broader strokes that fold over the rice and noodles.

Deep-frying Whatever you're deep-frying, make sure to start with enough vegetable oil to cover the ingredients. I like using either a wok or deep pot for deep-frying. Once you get the hang of this technique, you'll never have to worry about burnt or uncooked food again. Just remember a few simple rules. If you're deep-frying something like chicken with bone-in, then you don't want to set the temperature of the stove to anything higher than medium high and possibly lower than that if your stove has a strong heating capacity. Higher heat will result in browning and crisping exteriors quickly while interiors will remain relatively raw. A higher heat setting works for deep-frying dishes such as Banana Fritters (*Pisang Goreng*) because the banana is already cooked; you just want to brown and crisp the outside batter, which takes relatively little time. Conversely, an ingredient as substantial as chicken breast needs much longer cooking time at lower temperatures to ensure that the inside is thoroughly cooked while the outside doesn't burn too quickly. Also remember to allow the oil to come up to temperature before dropping in any ingredients otherwise you'll end up with a soggy, oily mess. A

good way to check if the oil is hot enough is by sticking a chopstick in the oil. If little bubbles surface around the chopstick, the oil should be hot enough.

Getting the Most Out of a Lime We've all experienced the great annoyance of buying limes that looked beautiful at the market only to get home and find that they're dried up. A good technique to getting the most juice out of a lime is to either microwave the lime for about 20 to 30 seconds or run it under hot water for a minute, then roll it around firmly with the palm of your hand on a cutting board. This yields a spectacular amount of juice from good limes and at least something out of a bad one. Save your taste buds and stay far away from all the pre-bottled versions, they're just not a good substitute.

Keeping Herbs Fresh By now, you realize how strongly I advocate using all fresh ingredients and there's no aspect of Indonesian cuisine that warrants that rule more than using fresh herbs. Most of us don't have the time to shop more than once a week so I use this technique to save time and cost, and prevent waste. As soon as you get home with fresh herbs, rinse each type in cold water and drain thoroughly. Using either a paper towel lined basket or baking sheet, spread the herbs gently and pat dry with another paper towel. Allow them to air dry completely for at least several hours up to overnight. Once they are thoroughly dried, store each type separately in zip lock bags lined with new sheets of paper towels.

Useful Tools and Utensils

Having the right tools for the job makes cooking a joy. Here are some items that I think make the whole Indonesian cooking experience easier, more enjoyable, and produce tastier results. Typically, Indonesian kitchens are simply outfitted, but it's difficult to argue that some modern conveniences can save time and hassle without affecting the quality of the food.

Asian Butcher Knife/Cleaver As cliché as it might sound, it's true that a dull knife is far more dangerous than a sharp one. I have experienced this myself, cutting my fingers in nasty accidents due to dull, low quality knives. I'm forever loyal to my Asian butcher knife with its huge rectangular shape and seemingly invincible steel heft. I know some of you may not be familiar or comfortable with this type of large knife but once you get used to its size and weight, you'll find it to be an extremely versatile and useful tool. I use this for everything from mincing garlic to cutting vegetables and chopping through all types of meats with bones. These knives can be purchased inexpensively at Asian grocery stores.

Asian Strainers There are many types of these strainers, the good ones feature some type of mesh-looking wire material in a rounded shape with a long wooden handle attached. Asian strainers are great for picking up noodles, vegetables, and anything you're either boiling or deep-frying that need to be drained. Make sure to purchase one with a long handle; it will save your skin from potential hazards while removing whatever you're cooking from its liquid. This tool beats using tongs for picking up noodles or something like shrimp chips where you're cooking a large quantity and need to drain them quickly. Certain recipe such as the Iced Coconut Cream with Jellies (page 114) require a particular kind of strainer which can be difficult to find in Western countries. The closest tool would be the ladle strainer, which looks just like a regular metal ladle but has small round holes.

Cutting Board An often-overlooked tool in kitchens is a strong, sturdy cutting board. Many Indonesian kitchens use large wooden butcher blocks as cutting boards, which is a great tool if you have a lot of space to thoroughly clean it and don't mind their weight. My preference is a large cutting board made of plastic or silicone with at least half an inch of depth. A good sized plastic cutting board will serve as a multi-purpose tool because you can use it for mincing herbs and spices; cutting vegetables and fruits; or chopping meats and seafood. Unlike wooden boards, you don't need to worry about bacteria seeping through its pores or the wood warping from water. Always clean your cutting boards with soap and hot water, allowing them to air dry thoroughly.

Food Processor In lieu of a traditional mortar and pestle, a modern day food processor is a fabulous tool. Besides grinding all types of herbs and spices that produce many of Indonesia's sambals and pastes, these nifty gadgets are a huge time saver when it comes to grinding all types of meats and mixtures. Were you so inclined, you could of course do everything the old-fashioned way and manually chop meat into its grounded state. While markets nowadays offer pre-ground meats, some recipes call for further fine grounding and mixing with other ingredients, which food processors complete in seconds. Like any other tool, investing in a good quality food processor will save on costs in the long run—a sturdy one should last for many years if not several decades.

Meat Pounder This is a tool that is not often discussed in Indonesian cooking but I have found it to be a great way to make perfectly cooked meats. For example, the recipe for Banjar Chicken Steak (page 65) calls for pan-frying chicken breasts. You can't always get perfectly shaped chicken breasts; one side is often much thicker than the other which means that cooking will be uneven. One side will be completely done cooking while the other is still raw on the inside. Using a meat pounder solves this issue easily. When using a meat pounder, I like to lay the meat across a plastic cutting board and cover it with a large piece of plastic wrap to protect from splattering bacteria all over the kitchen, other ingredients, and myself. With this method, you can then pound on the meat to whatever desired thickness without worrying about raw meat and its juices flying all over the place.

Metal Ladle A metal ladle with a long handle is necessary to work with soups and certain noodle dishes. Purchase one that's a good size with a sturdy handle, preferably one that is metal throughout or those with an outside layer of wood on the handle. Plastic ladles are never used in Indonesian cooking unless for serving desserts or cold dishes, and wooden ladles can often impart a strange flavor to the dish so should be avoided as well.

Mortar and Pestle (*Cobek or Ulek*) A traditional Indonesian mortar and pestle is one of the greatest kitchen tools of all time. Unlike those from other countries, Indonesia's version is flatter and more open on top, like a plate with rounded edges rather than an enclosed bowl-like contraption. The pestle is also shaped differently, having a distinctive curvature for ease of grip allowing for Indonesia's unique technique of grinding. Made of basalt stone, the Indonesian mortar and pestle allows herbs and spices to have optimum surface area contact with the rough stone that produces the delicious and spicy sambals with their smooth texture. Typically heavier than their Thai or Mexican counterparts, the Indonesian mortar and pestle is more readily available in Western regions in recent years. These should never be washed with soap of any kind but rather rinsed thoroughly with warm water and allowed to completely air dry before storing.

Rice Cooker One of the easiest tools to use in an Indonesian kitchen is a good quality rice cooker. I can't imagine any modern day kitchen without one; it saves on time, cleanup, and effort while cooking perfect, fluffy rice. You should follow the general instructions of your particular rice cooker though my personal rule of thumb for perfect white rice is 2 parts water to 1 part uncooked rice. These days you can find all types of rice cookers with price tags ranging from as low as $15 to as high as several hundred dollars. For the average home kitchen a rice cooker somewhere in the middle range does just fine. It does pay in the long run to invest in at least a decent rice cooker rather than the cheapest one because this is a tool that should last you for years. The great thing about modern day rice cookers is that you can just set the rice to cook and it will stay warm from at least a few hours to a few days (for the more expensive models) and you never have to worry about burning the rice or water over-flowing.

Wok (*Wajan*) One of the most invaluable tools in an Indonesian kitchen is

of course, the wok. The type of wok you need depends on whether you have an electric or gas range. Home cooks with gas stoves are lucky because nothing surpasses the quality or speed of a real fire. However, with the proper tools, you can create great dishes on either type of stove. If you have a gas stove, you can use the traditional and original cast iron wok with its rounded bottom. Make sure to find one with a long, sturdy handle on one side rather than the two short handles on either side. Unless you're a professional wok chef, working without a handle will be extremely difficult. Depending on the exact shape of your gas stove, you may also need a wok ring to stabilize it. For those of you with an electric stove, you'll do best with a carbon steel wok with a flat bottom so it can sit properly on the range. This too should have a long, sturdy handle. When purchasing a wok, don't be afraid to look it over carefully and run your hands all over it, roughly yanking at the parts to ensure that it is in fact, a sturdy model. There are plenty of people who have all types of fancy methods of caring for a wok but most of those steps are really unnecessary for modern day woks. If you're handling a brand new wok, simply pour a few tablespoons of vegetable oil on a paper towel and rub thoroughly all over the inside of the wok. Place the wok on the stove over high heat until smoke rises. Tilt the wok in every direction so all parts of the wok come into contact with the heat. Do this for just a couple of minutes.

Remove the wok from the heat and cool. Once it has cooled, rinse thoroughly under warm water and air dry. Once you begin using the wok regularly, make sure to use a soft sponge to clean with soap and water. Never use harsh bristles or any type of steel wool sponge. When working with the carbon steel type woks, also make sure to use only wooden or silicone spatulas and never metal ones that can scrape and ruin the wok.

Wooden Spatula With many Indonesian recipes calling for stir-frying techniques, it's essential to have at least one very sturdy and good quality wooden spatula. These come in various shapes and sizes; any of them are fine as long as they feature a long enough handle, a wide enough surface area and are sturdy.

Buying the Right Ingredients

I've always been a proponent of fresh and authentic ingredients in order to recreate the dishes of Indonesia. The following are some key ingredients for the typical Indonesian meal. Although these ingredients are slowly finding their way into many grocery stores, I have provided substitutes for those that are still difficult to find.

Bird's-Eye, Chili Pepper (*Cabe Rawit*) Amongst the spicier peppers, coming in at 100,000 to 225,000 on the Scoville heat scale, these peppers are typically harvested when they are about one-inch long and range from a bright green hue to a beautiful, deep red when mature. As with all peppers, the heat is found most intensely in the seeds, although this pepper packs a punch just in its skin alone. Widely used in stir-fries and curries, these tiny peppers are indispensable to Indonesians when making chili pastes, or sambals. Traditional methods of making sambals involve using a mortar and pestle to mash bird's eye chili peppers with fresh garlic. You can find these in the fresh produce section of a well stocked grocery store. You can substitute Dry Ground, Chili Peppers (see this page) if you can't find them fresh.

Coconut Milk (*Santen*) Coconut milk is indispensable to Indonesian cooking. A large variety of coconut milk can be found in western markets these days, which include brands from Thailand, Vietnam, and even Cuban companies based in Miami. They are found in cans, occasionally in cartons, and in powder form. Any of them are fine to use in Indonesian cooking. You can find coconut milk in the Ethnic food sections of most grocery stores. It will keep for a few days in the refrigerator if covered.

Coriander, Ground (*Bubuk Ketumbar*) A vital ingredient in many stews and soups in Indonesian cooking, ground coriander has a somewhat citrusy and nutty flavor. Not a spice with a particularly overwhelming fragrance or taste, it's easy to overlook its use until you notice that something isn't quite right in a dish. Ground coriander is one of those subtle ingredients that serves as a key accent in the balance of complex flavors without screaming its presence aloud. Commonly sold in both western and Asian markets in either small bottles or plastic pouches found in the spices section. Ground coriander should be stored in a cool, dry space.

Dry Ground, Chili Peppers (*Bubuk Cabe*) Several species of chili peppers are used in the production of the dry ground version, depending on the nation of origin. Red bird's eye chili peppers are often used to make this spicy condiment. The peppers are dried out under the sun, then either mashed up into the powder or ground up using a food processor. Dry ground chili pepper is a fantastic substitute for the fresh peppers not always available in the West. These days American supermarkets carry some type of Dry Ground Chili Pepper. Chinese versions typically use a wok-roasted method, lending a slightly burnt aroma, while Indonesian, Thai, and Vietnamese versions are spicier and smoother in texture. All Asian grocery stores carry various versions of Dry Ground Chili Peppers. Store in a cool dry space.

Dried Shrimp Paste (*Terasi*) These days it seems that every Southeast Asian nation has produced its own version of dried shrimp paste, each with an individual texture, odor, and flavor. In general, they can be interchanged in recipes, but try to use the Indonesian version when cooking Indonesian cuisine. Indonesian shrimp paste is known as *terasi*, which is typically sold in small blocks covered in a plastic wrapping. Shrimp paste (and the Malaysian shrimp paste known as *belachan*) is so tightly packed that, unlike the Thai version of shrimp paste, it is a hard block that requires cutting with a knife before using. Boasting a beautiful, dark aubergine hue, shrimp paste has the strongest, most full-bodied aroma when cooked compared to its other Asian counterparts. Indonesian shrimp paste is not always readily available in the West so, when necessary, substitute with the more easily found Thai shrimp paste, which typically comes in a white plastic tub with a red cap.

Galangal (*Lengkuas*) In the same family as the ginger root, galangal is often confused with ginger or turmeric due to their similar exteriors. Galangal boasts the lightest skin amongst the root family, though unlike ginger, it typically has darker, thin brown rings along its root. On the inside, galangal is almost always the lightest in color amongst the roots, with a soft creamy yellow color. It is also one of the toughest roots to work with, requiring either a very sharp or heavy knife to cut through. Galangal has a soft camphor-menthol aroma and is used in Indonesian soups, lending a more intense heat similar to ginger. Galangal can be found as whole roots in Asian grocery stores and often in its powder form. Stored tightly in resealable plastic bags, it can be kept in the freezer for several months.

Garlic (*Bawang Putih*) Indonesian cuisine would not be as profoundly rich or aromatic without garlic. Used extensively throughout Indonesia, garlic is one of the most popular ingredients in the country. Its most typical use is either in a finely minced form for cooking or mashed as part of sauces and sambals. Garlic's role in Indonesian cuisine is varied, ranging from dominant to subtle. Garlic cloves are available everywhere in both western and Asian supermarkets in the produce sections. They should be stored in a cool, dark place and allowed to breathe. They can be frozen but fresh garlic is optimal.

Ginger (*Jahe*) Ginger root finds it origins in Asia and is central to Indonesian cuisine. Similar in appearance to turmeric, ginger is a hard root with light to medium brown skin. Its flesh differs from turmeric though, with a light golden color when at its peak stage. Ginger's pungent, spicy base lends heat to stir-fries and soups, in addition to its delicate aroma. Ginger is used in savory dishes and also in desserts and warm teas. Young ginger imparts the greatest amount of sweet juice while stale ginger should be avoided. You can tell if ginger is too old by pressing firmly on it;

if it is too hard and doesn't give off a faint aroma, it is probably stale and will taste bitter. It can typically be found in the produce section of grocery stores. They can be stored in the refrigerator in a paper bag for a few weeks. They can also be peeled and sliced and stored in a jar of sherry.

Kaffir Lime Leaves (*Daun Jeruk Purut*) These leaves add an unmistakably fresh aroma to Indonesian cuisine. Used in many soups and stir-fries, kaffir lime leaves are unique and impossible to substitute. The leaves are used both fresh and dried. Stored in the freezer in air tight bags, these leaves can last a remarkably long time, retaining their flavor and scent. They can be found in the frozen food section of Asian grocery stores or purchased through online retailers.

Lemongrass (*Serai*) In the past decade or so lemongrass has become more widely available in the western hemisphere. This has made creating authentic Indonesian dishes much easier. In western supermarkets, lemongrass is usually available in the produce section in an already finely minced paste sold in plastic tubes. In Asian supermarkets, lemongrass comes in a larger variety of forms, ranging from its entire original stalk to finely minced and even thinly sliced (the latter two usually packaged in small plastic tubs). The refreshing and light citrus essence of lemongrass is difficult to mimic, but some cooks will substitute with lime zest. They will store in the refrigerator for up to three weeks, or can be frozen for up to 6 months without losing their flavor.

Limes (*Jeruk Nipis*) An easy to find ingredient, limes are a staple in Indonesian cuisine, used in cooking and in food presentations as a garnish. Bursting with freshness, limes exert a tangy bite, a welcome addition to heavier dishes or hot soups. Most Indonesian stews and soups arrive at the table with lime wedges on the side, brightening the complex flavors of these meals. Limes are also used in fresh sauces and condiments as opposed to their mass production counterparts that use vinegar to cut costs. A good lime should have a smooth texture, a uniformly green vibrant color and should be somewhat soft to the touch. Found in the fresh produce section of your grocery store, they will stay good for a week or two before they start to lose their flavor. They can't be frozen.

Nutmeg (*Pala*) Indigenous to the Banda Islands of Indonesia, nutmeg is widely used around the world, particularly in western desserts. Few realize its roots are in fact in Asia, from a species of the evergreen tree that produces both nutmeg and mace. Lending a low-toned, aromatic fragrance and distinctive sweet base, it is used sparingly in Indonesian cuisine as a subtle but key accent. Many Indonesian dishes influenced by the Dutch colonization feature nutmeg as an important ingredient. When recipes call for nutmeg, use either freshly ground nutmeg or already ground nutmeg. It's readily available in the spice section of grocery stores. Store in a cool dry place.

Bakmi Kuning   Somen   Bihun   Glass Noodles

Dried Egg Noodles, (*Bakmi Kuning*) As its names suggests, this variety of noodles is made from eggs and wheat. Influenced by the Chinese population, egg noodles are commonly used in Indonesian cooking and have become so popular through the generations that large business empires of pre-seasoned noodles and restaurants have been founded upon this one larger than life ingredient. In the West, Asian grocery stores carry a large variety, though the Chinese brands tend to dominate. Any type is fine for Indonesian cooking, though my personal favorites are those that closely resemble the ones found at my favorite noodle restaurant in Indonesia these are curly and come packaged in small rounds. These dried egg noodles are not to be confused or substituted for the kind typically sold in Western markets because these have a completely different taste, texture, and size.

Misoa (*Somen*) Thanks to the Chinese influence in Indonesia, Misoa noodles or *somen*, are a popular noodle that's used mostly in soups. Misoa are white, thin noodles boasting a very mild, gentle flavor, and soft texture thanks to the stretching it undergoes during production. When cooking with Misoa, it's important to remember that these noodles absorb so much liquid and so maintaining a proportion of the noodles and soup is crucial to the success of the dish. Commonly sold in Asian markets along with other dry noodles and usually near the soba buckwheat noodles, it is typically packaged in already portioned bunches.

Rice Stick, Noodles (*Bihun*) Rice stick noodles are known in the West by several names, such as thin rice noodles, rice vermicelli, or chow fun. Made from rice, *Bihun* is very different from the heavier and richer egg noodles. A wide variety of rice noodles are sold in Asian markets and it's important to purchase the right type. Some brands from China produce rice noodles that appear slightly curly and in my experience, those yield flavorless and rubbery noodles. The ones to look for have a uniform off-white coloring and are typically packaged in large bunches with a smooth, even texture throughout. Do not confuse rice noodles with the clearer mung bean noodles, (known in Indonesia as *Soun*) or the larger sized varieties of Vietnamese rice noodles used for *Pho*.

Cellophane, Noodles Also known as glass noodles, these are made from the starch of mung beans (or other bean products) and, as the name implies are glassy in appearance. They are highly absorbent and will pick up the flavors of the dish. Be careful when cooked with oil because the absorbent qualities can make them greasy.

Indonesian Palm Sugar (*Gula Jawa*)
This type of palm sugar is also known as *Gula Merah*, or red sugar, and is one of the most misinterpreted ingredients in the West. This is a dense sugar derived from the palmyra palm but is extremely different from palm sugars typically sold in western markets. While the western varieties of palm sugar are also hard and dense, they are a light to dark brown in color and less moist than Javanese sugar. Javanese sugar has an earthy aroma and deep sweetness with a color closely resembling molasses. In Asian markets in the West I've only encountered one type of Indonesian Javanese sugar sold and those are in cylindrical shapes covered in white plastic wrap with the words "*Gula Jawa*" printed on the packaging. This wonderfully rich and full-bodied sugar is unique to Indonesia, its flavor and moist, crumbly texture has no imitators. When recipes call for Javanese sugar, it is best not to substitute. These days most Asian markets carry it, along with online Asian grocery stores. When absolutely necessary, substitute with dense, tightly packed dark brown sugar. Store in a cool dry place.

Peanuts (*Kacang*) Recipes calling for peanuts in Indonesian cuisine typically refer to the unsalted, raw version. In Indonesia, the raw nuts are widely sold in their original shells, while in the West, an easier to use the dry version that's readily available in plastic pouches already de-shelled. Many Indonesian dishes and condiments feature a bold, nutty flavor, making this an indispensable ingredient in an Indonesian kitchen. When working with the raw peanuts, it's important to dry roast them for a few minutes in a wok or heavy pan until they are lightly browned before going on to combine them with other ingredients. They store easily: three months in a dry place; six months in the refrigerator; indefinitely if wrapped in plastic and placed in a freezer.

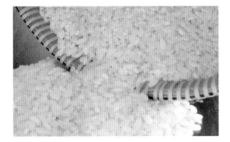

Rice (*Beras*) No other ingredient can be

a more vital in Indonesian cuisine than rice. Its raw form is known in Indonesia as *Beras*, while after cooking it is referred to as *nasi*. Indonesians love their rice, often eating the popular carbohydrate as many as three times a day. Though its usage can be found in the infamous dishes of *Nasi Goreng* (fried rice) and Chicken Porridge (*Bubur Ayam*), regular white rice reigns supreme as the staple of meals. The inclusion of white rice in meals is what allows Indonesians to enjoy so many savory and spicy dishes and condiments. Stews, curries, and stir-fries are also all eaten with white rice. In fact, the only time white rice is left out of a meal is when noodles take its place as the main starch. Found in the grains section of the grocery store, it should be stored in a cool, dry place.

Rose Syrup (*Sirup Mawar*) Rose syrup is an important ingredient in making many Indonesian drinks and desserts. With no remotely similar products anywhere in the world, its presence in recipes cannot be replaced. Boasting a deep red hue and a luxuriously thick consistency, rose syrup carries the fragrance of its namesake and translates into a distinctive floral sweetness on the palate. Produced only in Indonesia, a few brands of rose syrup can be found in Asian markets, though the Indonesian kind should not be confused with varieties from India. Those from India possess a completely different color, texture, and flavor that cannot be used in Indonesian cooking. All Indonesian brands selling rose syrup have unmistakable packaging—clear glass bottles that show the rich redness of the syrup and labeled "Rose Syrup" and/ or "*Sirup Mawar.*" Keep in a dry place or refrigerate.

Sambal Oelek When cooking Indonesian cuisine outside of Indonesia, ready-made Sambal Oelek is an invaluable ingredient that adds a tangy spiciness and a rich texture to dishes because of the seeds. Traditionally made with red chili peppers, Sambal Oelek typically has salt, sugar, and vinegar in it. The most widely available types are sold in clear, plastic bottles with bright green caps. All versions of Sambal Oelek are clearly marked with this name and should not be confused with the large variety of other spicy condiments such as sambal badjak or sambal terasi, many of which are sold side-by-side in Asian gro-cery stores. Using the Indonesian version of Sambal Oelek is preferred, however, it can be difficult to find in American markets. Substituting any Thai or Chinese version is fine as long as the product is clearly marked with the words "Sambal Oelek." Store in the refrigerator after opening.

Shallots (*Bawang Merah*) Of the onion family, shallots are mistakenly believed to originate in Asia, this is not surprising considering its wide usage in most Asian cuisines. In Indonesia, shallots are commonly used both in cooking and in the popular condiment, *Acar*. With a milder and sweeter flavor than regular onions, shallots add a subtle sweetness to dishes, as well as lending a chunkier texture in most of the pastes that are the foundation of many Indonesian stews, curries, and stir-fries. Shallots are readily available in the produce sections of both western and Asian markets. They keep fresh for a couple of months if stored in a dry area.

Sweetened Condensed, Milk (*Susu Manis*) Used sparingly in drinks and desserts, sweetened condensed milk has found popularity throughout Indonesia. Produced from cow's milk that has sugar added and water removed, condensed milk has a thick, molasses-like consistency with a creamy, light yellow color. Richly sweet, this ingredient is used mostly as a drizzle over Indonesian desserts and as a sweetener in iced beverages or hot coffee. Sweetened condensed milk is easily found in both western and Asian grocery stores, sold in cans that can remain fresh in the pantry for years if stored unopened. Once opened, it's best to transfer the condensed milk to a squeeze bottle to stay fresh longer in the refrigerator and for ease of use.

Tamarind Concentrate (*Asem*) Indonesians use large amounts of tamarind in many dishes, primarily in soups. In earlier years, fresh tamarind pulp was used to flavor dishes but these days it's easier to use the concentrated version that's readily available in Asian markets as well as some western stores. Tamarind lends a piquant sourness to dishes, along with a beautiful, rich brown hue. Tamarind concentrates available in the West possess a thick consistency similar to tomato ketchup, allowing for a thicker consistency when used in soups and stir-fries. More powerful than lime or lemon, the unique flavor of tamarind should not be substituted. It can be kept covered in a refrigerator for up to a year.

Soy Sauce (***Kecap Asin***) A very familiar product in the West, regular soy sauce has become a staple in most American supermarkets. Used frequently in Indonesian cooking, regular soy sauce is an essential part of an Asian pantry. Most soy sauce varieties across Asia have the same consistency and salty flavor so there is no issue in substituting one brand for another. Asian grocery stores in the West carry a large variety of soy sauce brands while Western markets tend to feature Japanese brands such as Kikkoman. My personal favorite line of soy sauces is from the Lee Kum Kee brand, they have a large variety that includes low sodium options and different experimental textures for home cooks who are already familiar with Indonesian cuisine.

Sweet Soy Sauce (***Kecap Manis***) Sweet soy sauce is another ingredient that is constantly found in Indonesian cooking. Less salty than regular soy sauce, sweet soy sauce is thick and black with a rich sweetness. Used in both cooking and as the main ingredient in many sauces, several varieties of sweet soy sauce can be found in Asian markets. Good-quality Indonesian sweet soy sauce includes brands like Cap Sate and Kecap Bango. However, the Indonesian brands can often be difficult to find so, when necessary, substitute with the easily found Lee Kum Kee brand of sweet soy sauce.

Soy Sauce   **Sweet Soy Sauce**

Tempeh In recent years, Tempeh, produced from nutrient and fiber rich soybeans, has gained popularity in the West as a protein super food. Indigenous to Indonesia, a natural culturing and fermentation process condenses soybeans into a cake-like form making Tempeh. This unusual ingredient can be easily found in the produce section of most western markets as well as Asian stores. It can keep in the refrigerator for a week or so; if frozen it can be kept for six months.

Turmeric (***Kunyit***) Part of the ginger family, turmeric is a root with a light to medium colored brown skin and a rich yellow-orange inside. This is one of the most widely used ingredients in Indonesian cooking as part of curries, soups, and rice dishes. Turmeric has an earthy flavor, subtle on the palate and scent.

Water Spinach or Morning Glory (***Kangkung***) Water Spinach is one of the most popular vegetables in Indonesia with its

powerful nutrients, including Vitamins K and C, folic acid, calcium, and fiber. In recent years, water spinach can be easily found in most Asian grocery stores in the fresh produce section, though it may be labeled as one of its many other alter egos. When cooking with water spinach the hard, rough edges of the stems should be trimmed off. People in the West like to discard the entire stems using only the leaves, but in Indonesia the entire vegetable is used after removing the ends. The thicker parts of the stalk are cut off from the leafy parts so they can be stir-fried first to soften. A good alternative to water spinach is a similar vegetable known as potato leaves. Water Spinach is highly perishable and needs to be used right away.

Sambal Dipping Sauces

Indonesians rarely eat a meal or even indulge in a savory snack without some type of spicy chili paste (sambal) or sauce. From fiery Shrimp Paste Chili Sauce (Sambal Terasi) to sweet and thick Sweet Soy Dip (Sambal Kecap Manis), this chapter introduces Indonesia's most popular condiments that are widely used for salads, main dishes, and snacks. Though Indonesians typically prepare sambals and sauces using a traditional stone mortar and pestle, these recipes include the quick and easy method of using a food processor to create the same intense flavors.

Peanut Satay Dip
Sambal Kacang

Indonesia is well known for its many dishes and sauces that feature peanuts. This Peanut Satay Dip is used as an accompaniment to grilled meats on skewers (satay) as well as on several types of salads. The recipe is quite simple but requires a little more time compared to other Indonesian sauces. This sauce will keep for months when stored in an airtight container in the refrigerator.

MAKES 1½ CUPS (375 ML)
PREPARATION TIME: 5 MINUTES
COOKING TIME: 10-20 MINUTES DEPENDING ON HEATING CAPACITY OF THE STOVE

¼ cup (50 g) peanuts, unsalted and raw
6 cloves garlic
1 stalk lemongrass, inner part of thick bottom third, peeled and minced
2 tablespoons oil
2 cups (500 ml) coconut milk
¼ teaspoon cayenne pepper
½ teaspoon salt
1½ teaspoons sugar

1 Dry roast the peanuts over high heat in a small wok or skillet, shaking the nuts around every few minutes. The peanuts should be a rich, dark brown color when done. This process will take anywhere from 5 to 15 minutes depending on the heating capacity of the stove.
2 Using a mortar and pestle or a food processor, grind the roasted peanuts, garlic cloves, and lemongrass until it's very smooth. Return the paste to the hot wok or skillet with the 2 tablespoons of oil and sauté for 2 to 3 minutes over medium high heat until fragrant and golden.
3 Add the coconut milk, cayenne pepper, salt, and sugar, stirring until thoroughly mixed. Allow the mixture to come to a vigorous simmer then remove from the heat. Allow the peanut sauce to cool.

Sweet Soy Dip
Sambal Kecap Manis

Sweet Soy Dip is a versatile condiment and is widely used in Indonesian cuisine. For those of you who have had the opportunity to visit Indonesia, you may be familiar with this sauce from eating the grilled meats on skewers (satay). However, this sauce is also used extensively for grilled and deep-fried seafood dishes. When properly stored, the sauce can be kept for several months.

MAKES 1½ CUPS (375 G)
PREPARATION TIME: 10 MINUTES

1 cup (250 ml) sweet soy sauce
3 shallots, thinly sliced
2-4 bird's eye chili peppers, finely chopped
1 small fresh tomato, finely diced

Mix all the ingredients together well in a bowl until smooth. This sauce is typically used for all types of meat skewers and roasted meats.

Tomato Chili Sauce

Sambal Tomat

Similar to Shrimp Paste Chili Sauce, Tomato Chili Sauce uses nearly all the same ingredients with the exception of the shrimp paste. Light in flavor and soft in texture, this chili sauce is widely used to accompany fried appetizers and main dishes. The absence of shrimp paste in this version makes it a more versatile companion to other foods. This sauce should be consumed within a few days because the fresh tomatoes will spoil quickly.

MAKES 1½ CUPS (375 ML)
PREPARATION TIME: 5 MINUTES
COOKING TIME: 3-5 MINUTES

5-7 cloves garlic
2 shallots
4-5 bird's-eye chili peppers, rinsed and ends trimmed
½ tablespoon oil
1 large tomato, rinsed and chopped into chunks
1 teaspoon salt
1 teaspoon sugar

1 Grind the garlic, shallots, and chili peppers using a mortar and pestle or food processor until a smooth paste forms.
2 Heat the oil in a small pan over medium high heat and sauté the paste for about 1 minute until very fragrant and lightly charred. Add the tomatoes, salt, and sugar. Sauté until the tomato has broken down slightly. Transfer to serving bowl and, if necessary, use a fork to break down the tomato chunks further. Serve warm.

Shrimp Paste Chili Sauce
Sambal Terasi

No other spicy sauce embodies Indonesia more than Shrimp Paste Chili Sauce. This condiment is not for the faint of heart nor for novices to extremely spicy foods. Shrimp Paste Chili Sauce is my all time favorite chili sauce. Thanks to lots of garlic and shrimp it's got some amazing and strong flavors. Indonesians serve this as a condiment to many fried foods as well as a dipping sauce for raw vegetables.

MAKES 1½ CUPS (125 G)
PREPARATION TIME: 10 MINUTES
COOKING TIME: 1 MINUTE

¼ tablespoon oil
½ tablespoon dried shrimp paste (Indonesian *terasi* or Thai shrimp paste)
4-5 cloves garlic
¼ teaspoon salt
½ teaspoon sugar
8 bird's-eye chili peppers, rinsed and ends trimmed

1 Heat the oil in a small pan over high heat and sauté the dried shrimp paste for about 30 to 45 seconds, mashing thoroughly until the unmistakably pungent scent permeates the air. Set aside to cool.
2 Grind the garlic, salt, and sugar in a mortar and pestle or food processor until smooth. Add the chili peppers and shrimp paste to the grinder and continue to grind until all the ingredients are thoroughly combined and have a smooth texture. Shrimp Paste Chili Sauce should be eaten on the same day it's made and not kept overnight.

Chapter One

Appetizers and Snacks

Snacking is one of the Indonesian people's greatest passions. The appetizers included in this chapter range from foods eaten as part of a larger meal to barbecued meats that are treated as an anytime favorite. A beautiful array of flash-fried fresh vegetables results in crispy and savory treats, while the sweet soy marinades make the barbecued beef and chicken succulent and juicy. Whether you are interested in a simple starter or a more complex offering, Indonesian appetizers are an exotic way to begin any meal.

Pan-fried Soybean Cakes Tempeh Goreng

Packed with nutrients and fiber, this Indonesian staple is a great appetizer for any day of the week or as part of a cultural dinner party. *Tempeh* used to be difficult to find but within the past few years even mainstream American supermarkets have begun to carry this healthful product in their produce department. *Tempeh* is made only in Indonesia and is always sold in long, rectangular shapes. Typically, they're about half an inch (12 mm) in thickness, three inches wide (8 cm) by seven or eight inches long (20 cm). In the West, *tempeh* is sold in either clear plastic packaging labeled "*tempeh*" or in dark green banana leaves similarly labeled. This recipe is super easy and quick, resulting in a crisp, salty exterior, perfect for dipping with a sweet and spicy sauce like sambal oelek or Shrimp Paste Chili Sauce.

MAKES 10-12 PIECES
PREPARATION TIME: 5-6 MINUTES
COOKING TIME: 3 MINUTES

Oil for deep-frying
1 package of *tempeh* (8 oz/250 g)
Sprinkling of water
2 teaspoons garlic powder
1¼ teaspoons salt

CONDIMENT
Sambal oelek or Shrimp Paste Chili
Sauce (page 23)

1 Heat the oil in a large wok or deep pot over medium high heat.
2 Slice the *tempeh* thinly on the diagonal so you have a somewhat rectangular shape, like a parallelogram. Place the sliced tempeh in a mixing bowl and gently sprinkle bits of water over all the *tempeh*.
3 Evenly dust both sides of the *tempeh* slices with the garlic powder and salt. Allow it to marinate for 5 minutes while waiting for the oil to come up to temperature.
4 Gently place a few of the *tempeh* in the oil and fry for 2 to 3 minutes on each side until golden brown. Drain on a paper towel. Serve warm with sambal oelek or Shrimp Paste Chili Sauce.

Corn and Shrimp Fritters Bakwan Jagung

Corn and Shrimp Fritters used to be sold on the streets but it's become more of an authentic home-cooked snack these days. Indonesians' love of fried foods is evidenced by this savory treat with a mix of fresh, sweet corn kernels and tiny shrimp in a moist batter with a golden brown finish. This appetizer is fabulous for intimate, informal gatherings rather than larger formal parties, because they can be a little messy to eat. These are absolutely delicious when served with a variety of spicy sauces.

MAKES 12 FRITTERS
PREPARATION TIME: 5-7 MINUTES
COOKING TIME: 4 MINUTES

Oil for deep-frying
½ lb (250 g) small salad shrimp, raw
2 cups (200 g) shredded cabbage and carrots (coleslaw mix)
2 cups (3 cobs/200 g) corn kernels
2 green onions (scallions), cut into ½ in (12 mm) diagonals
1½ tablespoons Fried Garlic (see right)
3 large eggs
2 teaspoons salt
½ teaspoon white pepper
1½ cups (300 g) all-purpose flour
1½ cups (375 ml) water

1 Heat the oil in a wok or deep frying pan over medium high heat.
2 Place all the ingredients in a large mixing bowl and using a spatula or hands, mix everything thoroughly but gently. Scoop the mixture using a medium sized ladle and gently pour into the hot frying oil, be careful to not let the batter spread out too far.
3 Fry a few fritters at a time, using a medium sized ladle as a measuring tool. Take care to leave space between the fritters and not to overcrowd the wok. Overcrowding will lower the temperature of the oil and result in soggy fritters. Fry the fritters approximately 1 to 2 minutes on each side until golden brown. Remove with a slotted spoon.
4 Drain the fritters on a paper towel and after they have drained, serve with a sauce of your choice.

Fried Garlic

1 cup finely minced garlic
8 tablespoons oil

1 Heat the oil on medium high heat in a skillet or small wok. Toss in the minced garlic and stir-fry for a few minutes, allowing the garlic to rest briefly every few seconds. They are done when golden brown and crisp. Drain on paper towels.
2 Once they are completely air-dried, either use as a garnish immediately or place in an air-tight container. If stored properly, the Fried Garlic can last several months.

Chicken and Potato Croquettes Croket Ayam

Countries around the world, from Malaysia to Cuba, have their distinctive version of croquettes. Indonesia is no exception, with its mouth-watering interpretation of warm potato croquettes, thanks to the Dutch influence from a bygone era. While this recipe does require a little time and preparation, the readily available ingredients and spectacular results make it all worthwhile. Fabulous for get-togethers or large parties, these Chicken and Potato Croquettes can be made in advance, frozen, and kept for a long time before frying. Across Indonesia, roadside stalls and mom and pop restaurants have invented their own versions of the dipping sauce. I've included my grandmother's sauce here, one that finds its roots in the 300-year Dutch colonial presence in Indonesia.

MAKES 14
PREPARATION TIME: 35-45 MINUTES
COOKING TIME: 20-30 MINUTES

5 medium potatoes, (1½ lb/750 g) peeled
    and cut into small chunks
¼ lb (100 g) ground or minced chicken
½ teaspoon salt each for the chicken,
    potatoes, and bread crumbs (total 1½
    teaspoons)
¼ teaspoon ground white pepper
¼ teaspoon ground nutmeg
¼ teaspoon ground coriander
1 cup (200 g) breadcrumbs
¼ teaspoon garlic powder
¼ teaspoon onion powder
Oil for deep-frying
All-purpose flour for dusting
2 large eggs, whisked

CROQUETTE DIPPING SAUCE
3 tablespoons mayonnaise
1 tablespoon sambal oelek
1¼ tablespoons Dijon mustard
¼ teaspoon salt

1 Bring several inches of water to a vigorous boil in a medium sized pot over high heat. Boil the potato chunks for 10 to 15 minutes until fork tender. Drain and place the potatoes in a large bowl. Using a masher or large fork, mash the chunks with ½ teaspoon of salt until they become smooth. Set aside to cool down.

2 Mix the ground chicken with ½ teaspoon of salt, white pepper, ground nutmeg, and ground coriander. Dry sauté the chicken in a nonstick skillet over high heat until thoroughly cooked. Set aside in a bowl to cool down.

3 Mix the breadcrumbs in a medium sized bowl with ½ teaspoon of salt, garlic powder, and onion powder thoroughly.

4 Once the potatoes and chicken have completely cooled down, assemble the potatoes, chicken, and flour next to each other for dusting. Also have a large baking pan lined with aluminum ready for placing the croquettes. First dust your hands thoroughly with flour. Then take about 2 large spoonfuls of the mashed potatoes in your left hand and press down in the middle to create a somewhat round indentation. Place a small amount of the ground chicken in the round indentation. Using a gentle squeezing motion with your left palm along with help from your flour-dusted right hand fingers, close the mashed potatoes over the chicken. Gently form a short log-like shape by rolling the croquette between your palms, taking care so it doesn't break and that the chicken is completely covered by the potatoes. Dust with more flour whenever necessary. Place the shaped croquette on the aluminum lined baking sheet. Repeat until all the ingredients are used.

5 Heat the oil in a wok or large pot over high heat (the setting just below the highest).

6 Place the egg wash, breadcrumbs, and tray of croquettes near each other and by the wok of heating oil. Dip the shaped croquettes in the egg wash thoroughly, then into the breadcrumbs, making sure to coat completely. Slip the croquette into the hot oil and fry until golden brown all over, just about 30 seconds to 1 minute. Flip the croquettes over after the first 20 seconds or so. Fry 4 to 5 croquettes at a time, but don't overcrowd. Drain the croquettes on a paper towel.

7 In a small bowl, mix all the ingredients for the Croquette Dipping Sauce and serve with the croquettes on the side.

Chicken Satays Sate Ayam

Chicken Satay is one of Indonesia's quintessential dishes. It is served across the country, from roadside stalls to elegant five-star hotels. These savory pieces of skewered chicken can be served as a simple weekday main entree or as a classy and exotic party appetizer. For this Indonesian version of an all-around Asian favorite, sweet soy sauce should not be substituted because its very distinctive flavor makes the whole dish wonderful. Any brand of Indonesian sweet soy sauce is acceptable or substitute with Lee Kum Kee Sweet Soy Sauce, which can be easily found in any Asian grocery store. This recipe uses a high broil in the oven to mimic the original barbecue used in Indonesia so that anyone with a regular kitchen can prepare this delectable tidbit. Those of you with a barbecue can follow the recipe as is just make sure to add a few tablespoons of oil to the marinade so the chicken doesn't stick to the grill.

MAKES 25-30 SKEWERS
PREPARATION TIME: 15-20 MINUTES
COOKING TIME: 8-12 MINUTES

30 bamboo skewers
3 boneless, skinless chicken breasts
 (1½ lb/ 750 g)
½ cup (125 ml) sweet soy sauce
½ cup (125 ml) coconut milk
1 teaspoon garlic powder
1½ teaspoons salt
Freshly ground black pepper

CONDIMENT
Sweet soy sauce

1 Soak the skewers in cold water for at least ½ an hour so they won't burn on the grill.
2 Rinse the chicken under cold water. Cut the chicken into small bite-size chunks and place in a large bowl. Mix in the sweet soy sauce, coconut milk, garlic powder, salt, and ground black pepper. Allow the chicken to marinate for at least ½ an hour (up to overnight).
3 Heat the oven to high broil.
4 Line a large baking sheet with aluminum foil. Slide 3 to 4 chicken pieces on each skewer and arrange on the baking sheet. Broil under high heat for 8 to12 minutes until the chicken is golden brown and just beginning to char on the edges.
5 Serve with sweet soy sauce on the side.

Beef Satays Sate Daging

From my early childhood, I remember the distant, familiar sounds of two pieces of wood knocking loudly against each other followed by the high pitched yell of the satay man. Every neighborhood in Indonesia has its own satay man, the expert beef griller who walks rapidly from one street to another with his makeshift "restaurant" on wheels. From a mile away you can smell the unmistakable caramelizing of meat with sweet soy sauce on the mobile charcoal grill. Even when my family had eaten dinner already, somehow, there was always room for Beef Satays. Just a snack, we would call it. And the satay man would be beckoned to our front gates where he would swiftly add skewer upon skewer of satay on a banana leaf before deftly drizzling both peanut and sweet soy sauce all over the grilled meat. With everyone scrambling to grab skewers from the plate, most of the satay was gone before even reaching the dining table, something that is certain to happen every time you make this savory appetizer.

MAKES 16-18 SKEWERS
PREPARATION TIME: 15-20 MINUTES
COOKING TIME: 8-12 MINUTES

18 bamboo skewers
1 lb (500 g) beef sirloin or ribeye
¼ cup (65 ml) sweet soy sauce
¼ cup (65 ml) soy sauce
1½ tablespoons oil

1 Soak the skewers in cold water for at least ½ an hour to prevent them from burning.
2 Cut the beef into small, bite-sized chunks. Put in a bowl and pour the soy sauce and sweet soy sauce over the beef chunks and mix well. Marinate for up to 1 hour.
3 Slide 3 to 4 chunks of beef on each water soaked skewer.
4 Heat ½ tablespoon of oil in a non-stick skillet or pan over medium high heat. Place 6 to 8 skewers (however many that will fit comfortably) in the skillet and pan fry for 3 to 4 minutes on each side. Repeat this last step for the remaining skewers, using the ½ tablespoon of oil for each set of skewers. Alternatively, you can cook the beef on an outdoor grill, making sure to baste the grill with oil so the skewers won't stick. Serve immediately.

Fresh Spring Rolls Lumpia Basah

In the Western hemisphere, spring rolls and fresh rolls have made their way into our common culinary vocabulary. Indonesian fresh rolls however, are very different from their counterparts from other Asian nations, featuring a thin, crepe-like exterior. Heavily influenced by the Dutch, this particular recipe is my grandmother's version of Indonesian fresh rolls. Light and savory, with a warm chicken and shrimp filling, these rolls do take a little time to prepare but are an excellent choice for cooking when entertaining. It's perfect for family gatherings.

Fresh Spring Rolls

MAKES 5 ROLLS
PREPARATION TIME: 45-50 MINUTES (INCLUDES ROLLING)
COOKING TIME: 7-10 MINUTES

BATTER FOR THE WRAPPERS
1 cup (200 g) all-purpose flour
1 large egg
1¼ cups (300 ml) water
¼ teaspoon salt
Olive oil for greasing the pan

LUMPIA FILLING
½ cup (100 g) green beans, finely chopped
½ head of cabbage, sliced thinly to make
    2 cups (500 g)
6-8 cloves garlic, minced
½ lb (250 g) ground or minced fresh boneless
    chicken meat
½ lb (250 g) small fresh shrimp, peeled,
    deveined, and finely chopped
1 tablespoon soy sauce
½ teaspoon salt
Freshly ground black pepper to taste
5 teaspoons Dijon mustard
2 tablespoons olive oil

1 In a large bowl, whisk together all the ingredients for the Batter except for the olive oil, until it's smooth and lump-free.

2 Heat a non-stick skillet over medium high heat. Coat with a dash of olive oil and pour a medium sized ladle of the Batter into the skillet. Quickly move the skillet around to coat it thinly with the Batter. Cook for approximately 30 to 40 seconds on each side. The wrappers will be a very light golden color with nearly no brown spots. Lay out each wrapper on a large baking sheet to cool down, making sure not to pile one on top of another to avoid sticking.

3 Bring 2 inches of water to a boil in a small pot, then remove from the heat. Place the chopped green beans and sliced cabbage into the hot water for 30 seconds and drain. Set aside.

4 Heat the olive oil in a wok or sauté pan over high heat and lightly brown the garlic. Add the ground chicken and sauté for about 1½ minutes. Add the shrimp and stir thoroughly for another 2 minutes or so until thoroughly cooked.

5 Combine the chicken and shrimp mixture with the green beans, cabbage, soy sauce, salt, and pepper in a large bowl. Toss together until well mixed and allow it to cool for 15 minutes.

6 To assemble the fresh rolls, place one wrapper on a serving plate and spread 1 teaspoon of mustard evenly all over the wrapper. Add a few spoons of the chicken mixture in the middle of the wrapper, leaving 1 inch on the left and right sides. Take the end of the wrapper closest to you and

fold over the mixture. Fold the left and right sides together over the middle, then gently roll it away from you until the roll is formed. Unlike other fresh rolls, this one is not meant to seal up. It's a little messy to eat but well worth it for the warm, savory goodness.

Savory Cucumber Relish Acar

Savory Cucumber Relish is a tangy, condiment used frequently in Indonesia to accompany meat dishes and appetizers. Most often used with meat on skewer (satay) appetizers in addition to the traditional Indonesian peanut dressing. Savory Cucumber Relish can be made several days in advance. It's best to seerve the Cucumber Relish in a bowl with a spoon since every one has their favorite way of eating this condiment, either by drizzling the marinade over their food or enjoying it as a separate dish with rice.

MAKES 3 CUPS (750 G)
PREPARATION TIME: 10 MINUTES

1 large cucumber, peeled and cubed
1 medium carrot, diced
½ cup (125 ml) white vinegar
1 teaspoon salt
4 tablespoons sugar

1 Mix all the ingredients together in a medium sized bowl until thoroughly combined and the sugar has dissolved.
2 Place the Savory Cucumber Relish in either a closed jar or tightly wrapped bowl and refrigerate at least overnight before serving. The longer you leave the relish to marinate, the better it tastes. Stored properly, it can last in the refrigerator for several weeks.

Chilied Eggs Sambal Telur

This recipe will turn ordinary eggs into an addictive appetizer or side dish. With a crispy skin and a sweet and spicy sauce drizzled over the top, these eggs always get a great reaction. Incredibly easy to prepare, the boiled eggs can be made ahead of time and kept until ready to deep fry. The sauce will also keep for up to a week in the refrigerator when tightly covered with plastic wrap or in a sealed container. Always make more of these than you think you need to because people can't resist them.

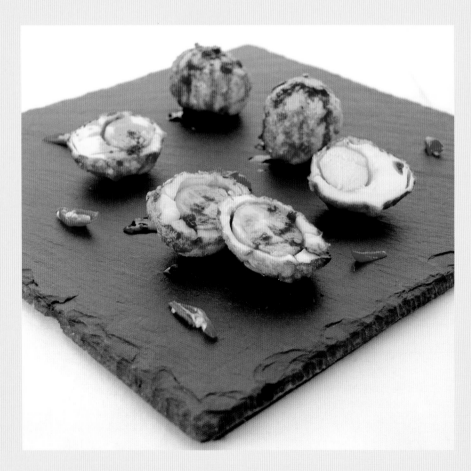

Oil for deep-frying
4 large eggs, hardboiled and shelled
⅛ teaspoon salt
2 tablespoons sweet soy sauce
1 tablespoon sambal oelek
1 tablespoon Fried Shallots (see below)

1 Heat the oil in a wok or deep pot over medium high heat.
2 Fry the hardboiled eggs for 2½ to 4 minutes until golden brown and crisp all around. Drain the eggs on a paper towel and let the eggs cool down for a few minutes.
3 In a small bowl, mix the salt, sweet soy sauce, and sambal oelek until thoroughly blended.
4 Slice the eggs lengthwise in half and arrange on a serving plate. Drizzle the sauce over the eggs. Garnish with a sprinkling of Fried Shallots.

Fried Shallots

1 cup thinly sliced shallots or approx. 7-8
   medium sized whole shallots
4 tablespoons oil

1 Heat the oil over medium high heat in a skillet or small wok. Toss in the sliced shallots and stir-fry for a few minutes, allowing the shallots to rest briefly every few seconds. Fry until they are golden brown and crisp. Drain on paper towels.
2 Once they are completely air-dried, either use as a garnish immediately or place in an air-tight container. If stored properly, Fried Shallots can last several months.

Spinach Tempura Kripik Bayam

Indonesians love to snack on pretty much everything and they've refined the art of turning the ordinary into something delectable and irresistible. Here, fresh spinach leaves are turned into a kind of tempura Indonesian style—crisp and flaky. Easy to prepare and popular with both kids and adults, Spinach Tempura is a fabulous staple as an appetizer and a great way to include some important nutrients in a tasty snack.

MAKES 20 CRISPS
PREPARATION TIME: 5 MINUTES
COOKING TIME: 2 MINUTES

Oil for deep-frying
Whites of 2 large eggs, and 1 yolk
4 tablespoons all-purpose flour
¼ cup (65 ml) soda water
20 large spinach leaves, rinsed and pat-
  ted completely dry with a paper towel
Salt for sprinkling

1 Heat the oil in a wok or deep frying pan over just a little lower than high heat.
2 Whisk together the 2 egg whites and yolk until they are smooth. Add the flour and soda water. Whisk again until blended thoroughly and smooth.
3 Dip each spinach leaf in the egg mixture thoroughly and gently slide into the oil. Fry the leaves on each side for a minute or so until golden brown. Drain on paper towels. Once all the leaves are fried and laid out together on the paper towel, sprinkle a dash of salt evenly over all the leaves. Serve immediately.

Savory Fish Cakes

Empek Empek Palembang

These fish cakes are called Empek Empek Palembang, which is one of the largest cities on the island of Sumatra in the north-western hemisphere of Indonesia. Pan-fried fish cakes have a chewy texture that contrasts well with the tangy, savory sauce. Traditionally, the fish cakes are served in the sauce, almost like a soup, rather than with the sauce on the side. Some versions of the dish also feature a small quantity of egg noodles, arranged in the sauce just beneath the fish cakes. In this recipe though, I've omitted the noodles to keep the dish on a lighter note.

1 lb (500 g) fresh tilapia fish fillets (or any white, tender fish)
6-10 cloves garlic
6 tablespoons ice water
1 large egg
¾ teaspoon salt
5 tablespoons cornstarch
Oil to coat the bottom of large frying pan

TANGY TAMARIND SAUCE
5 cups (1.25 liters) water
4 tablespoons tamarind concentrate
3 tablespoons dark brown sugar
6-10 cloves garlic
½ teaspoon ground red chili pepper
3 tablespoons small dried shrimp
¾ teaspoon salt

1 Cut the fish fillets into large chunks. Using a food processor, grind the fish, garlic, and ice water until a smooth, thick paste is formed. Transfer the paste into a large mixing bowl.
2 Add the egg, salt, and cornstarch to the paste, mixing everything thoroughly.
3 Coat the bottom of a large frying pan with oil and heat over medium high heat. Using your hands, take about 2 tablespoons of the fish mixture and shape into a somewhat flat (¼-inch/6 mm thick) round disc. Place gently into the oil to pan fry for 2 to 3 minutes on each side until golden brown. Continue this step until all the fish mixture has been pan-fried. Drain on a paper towel.
4 To make the Tangy Tamarind Sauce, combine the water, tamarind, and dark brown sugar in a medium sized pot and bring it to a vigorous boil over high heat.
5 Using a mortar and pestle or food processor, grind the garlic, ground chili pepper, and dried shrimp until smooth. Add to the boiling tamarind sauce and stir until thoroughly dissolved. Turn off the heat.
6 Arrange the fish cakes in serving bowls. Ladle the Tangy Tamarind Sauce over the fish cakes and serve immediately.

Crisp Tofu with Sweet Spicy Sauce Tahu Gejrot

When I'm far away from one of the places I consider home, I find myself missing certain dishes. Not the fancy, sophisticated ones served in the top hotels, but the everyday foods found in quaint little roadside stalls. Crisp Tofu with Sweet and Spicy Sauce is as down home and pedestrian as it gets. Deep fried tofu cubes come out fantastically crisp on the outside and hot and soft on the inside. Dipped in a lusciously sweet and spicy sauce, this is such a delicioius appetizer it's hard to believe that it is so easy to make.

SERVES 4   PREPARATION TIME: 5 MINUTES
COOKING TIME: 3-4 MINUTES

1½ lb (750 g) firm tofu, drained and cut into 1 in cubes
Oil for deep-frying

SWEET AND SPICY SAUCE
2-3 bird's-eye chili peppers
12-16 cloves garlic
1 medium shallot
2 tablespoons dark brown sugar
½ tablespoon salt plus extra for sprinkling
3 tablespoons sweet soy sauce
4 tablespoons water

1 Heat the oil in a wok or large pot over high heat. While the oil comes up to temperature, spread the tofu cubes on a large platter and pat gently on all sides with paper towels to soak up the remaining liquid.
2 Carefully slide as many tofu cubes as will fit into the wok or large pot without overcrowding. Deep-fry the tofu for 3 to 4 minutes until crisp. Make sure to gently turn the tofu cubes over about halfway through the cooking time. Drain on a paper towel.
3 Using a mortar and pestle or food processor, grind the chili peppers, garlic, shallot, dark brown sugar, and salt until smooth. Place the paste into a medium sized mixing bowl and add the sweet soy sauce and water. Stir until thoroughly mixed. Serve warm tofu cubes with the Sweet and Spicy Sauce drizzled on top or on the side as a dipping sauce.

Chapter Two

Soups

Indonesian soups showcase bold flavors and are filled with easy to find, nutritious ingredients. My personal favorites change from day to day—there are so many delicious soups, it's hard to decide. Indonesia's version of Chicken Noodle Soup (page 49) features thin cellophane noodles and tender pieces of shredded chicken with the summery scent of lemongrass in every bite. Oxtail Soup (page 41) is a must for meat lovers with the garlic and pepper infused oxtail meat falling off the bones and melting in your mouth. Some Indonesian soups are incredibly light and healthy, making them a perfect alternative to heavier meals while others are heavenly sinful, enjoyed as meals in themselves.

Lemongrass Chicken Soup

Sop Ayam Lengkuas

Lemongrass is one of the staple ingredients in Indonesian cooking, lending an aromatic freshness to every dish in which it's featured. In this mildly flavored soup, lemongrass plays a starring role, its unmistakably citrus flavor infuses the soup both in scent and taste. Some who've enjoyed this soup claim that the steam from the lemongrass helps in combating congestion problems. I say the savory goodness of this simple and delicate soup just makes people forget everything else. Light and nutritious, this is a perfect soup for anyone watching his or her cholesterol and caloric intake.

SERVES 4-6
PREPARATION TIME: 10 MINUTES
COOKING TIME: 20-25 MINUTES

7 cups (1.5 liters) chicken stock
3 cups (750 ml) water
1¼ lb (550 g) ground or minced fresh bone-less chicken meat
7-14 cloves garlic, finely minced
2 stalks lemongrass, tender inner part of bottom third only, minced
1 large egg
1 tablespoon soy sauce
¾ teaspoon salt + 1 teaspoon for the soup
Freshly ground black pepper to taste
1 teaspoon garlic powder
1 tablespoon cornstarch
½ tablespoon sugar
4-6 tablespoons coriander leaves (cilantro), roughly chopped

1 Bring the chicken stock and water to a vigorous boil in a medium sized pot over high heat.
2 Mix the ground chicken, minced garlic, minced lemongrass, egg, soy sauce, ¾ teaspoon salt, pepper, garlic powder, and cornstarch in a large bowl until thoroughly combined.
3 Place the mixing bowl near the boiling pot of stock. Using either a spoon or your hands, measure about 1 heaping tablespoon of the chicken mixture and form into a ball shape. Gently drop the chicken ball into the boiling stock. Repeat this step until all the chicken mixture is used up.
4 Add the remaining 1 teaspoon of salt and sugar into the stock, stirring gently. Once the chicken balls are floating on the top (just takes a few minutes), the soup is ready to serve. Garnish with chopped coriander leaves.

Oxtail Soup Sop Buntut

Decades ago Oxtail Soup was on every major hotel's menu in Indonesia. For whatever reason, recent years have seen a decline in its popularity. I've been fortunate enough to travel from western to eastern Indonesia, tasting a variety of interpretations of this soup by home cooks and small restaurant chefs. I've finally created what I believe is the original flavor of Oxtail Soup—full bodied, aromatic, and rich, as I had it during my childhood years. This recipe is quite simple to make, though requires a long stewing time. If you have a pressure cooker, cooking time can be reduced nearly in half.

SERVES 4
PREPARATION TIME: 10-15 MINUTES
COOKING TIME: 1½ HOURS TO 2 HOURS (SHORTER COOKING TIME IF USING PRESSURE COOKER)

6 quarts (6 liters) water
4 lb (2 kg) oxtail, rinsed
15-20 cloves garlic, smashed
3 large (3-in/8-cm) pieces ginger, peeled and smashed
16 star anise pods
2 teaspoons whole cloves
3 tablespoons ground coriander
1 tablespoon salt
1 teaspoon freshly ground black pepper, or to taste
4 tablespoons Fried Shallots (page 34)
4 green onions (scallions), roughly chopped

1 Bring the water to a vigorous boil in a large pot. Carefully lower the oxtail pieces into the boiling water and simmer over medium high heat for 30 minutes. Skim the foam off the top occasionally.
2 Add the garlic, ginger, star anise pods, cloves, ground coriander, salt, and pepper. Stir well. Simmer for another 1 to 1½ hour until the meat is extremely tender and falling off the bones.
3 Ladle the soup into serving bowls and garnish with chopped green onions and Fried Shallots. Serve hot with steamed rice.

Mushroom Medley Soup Sop Jamur

In all its complexity and variety of flavors, Indonesian cooking can often be deliciously simple, featuring fresh ingredients and easy techniques that showcase its bold and bright flavors. I learned the secret to this very simple Mushroom Medley Soup from a Japanese Indonesian chef at a hotel in Jakarta. I was fortunate enough to have tasted his soup and I was so overwhelmed by the light aroma and savory flavors that I had to ask him about his secret. As always, it comes down to using the finest, freshest ingredients available. Here is my version of this easy, quick, and incredibly nutritious soup.

SERVES 4
PREPARATION TIME: 10 MINUTES
COOKING TIME: 10 MINUTES

3 cups (750 ml) water
5 cups (1.25 liters) vegetable stock
2¾ cups (100 g) fresh shiitake mushroom
1¾ cups (100 g) fresh button mushroom
1¾ cups (100 g) fresh enoki mushroom
3 tablespoons soy sauce
¾ tablespoon salt
Juice of 1 whole lemon

1 Bring the water and vegetable stock to a vigorous boil in a medium sized pot over high heat.
2 Rub clean all of the mushrooms gently with a paper towel. Chop the mushrooms into bite-size pieces. Gently lower the mushrooms into the simmering stock.
3 Stir the mushrooms in the stock and lower the heat to medium high.
4 Spoon in the soy sauce, salt, and lemon juice. Combine until thoroughly mixed. Simmer for another 5 minutes and serve immediately.

Grandma's Tomato Soup

Sop Merah

When I could barely begin to read, I was already sifting through my mother's collection of recipes—those tattered books yellowed by the years and stained by countless cooking sessions in the family kitchen. My mother often turned to a particularly worn page that held my Grandma's Tomato Soup recipe, telling me stories of how my grandmother loved cooking this nutrient rich soup for the family, long before I was even born. Years later I would read that same page, filled with the youthful scrawls of the grandmother I never knew, wondering if I could recreate the lusciousness and bold flavors of her soup. I don't know if my version will ever have her special touch but whenever I do have Grandma's Tomato Soup on the stove, I like to think she's hovering over me, watching me cook for my loved ones just as she did so many years ago.

SERVES 4
PREPARATION TIME: 15-20 MINUTES
COOKING TIME: 30-40 MINUTES

9 cups (2 liters) water
1 large boneless, skinless chicken breast, rinsed (12 oz/350 g)
1 package (approx. 8 oz/250 g) button mushrooms
1 can (10 oz/330 g) Vienna sausages
2 tablespoons butter
6 shallots, minced (substitute ¼ red onion)
¼ cup (65 g) Italian flat-leaf parsley, chopped and allowing extra for garnish
2 tablespoons all-purpose flour
½ cup (125 ml) tomato ketchup
½ teaspoon salt
1 tablespoon sugar
4 tablespoons sweet soy sauce
1 teaspoon nutmeg
Freshly ground black pepper to taste
2 tomatoes, skin peeled and sliced thinly
2 large carrots, peeled and diced
Parsley, for garnish

1 Bring the water to a vigorous boil in a large pot. Place the chicken in the boiling water; boil for 5 minutes then turn the heat down to medium. Skim any foam off the top and continue to simmer.
2 Wipe the mushrooms clean with a paper towel; slice thinly and set aside.
3 Cut the Vienna sausages into small, bite-size chunks; set aside with the mushroom.
4 Heat the butter in a medium sized skillet or pan over high heat. Sauté the shallots and parsley until fragrant and translucent for just about 1 to 2 minutes; add the flour and mix well.
5 Combine the sautéed mixture into the chicken stock and stir well. Remove the chicken and chop it into small cubes; return the chicken to the pot.
6 Spoon in the ketchup, salt, sugar, sweet soy sauce, nutmeg, and pepper; stir well.
7 Gently toss in the sausage, mushrooms, tomatoes, and carrots. Stir well and let simmer for another 10 to 15 minutes. Serve hot with chopped parsley on top.

SERVES 4   PREPARATION TIME: 15-20 MINUTES
COOKING TIME: 30 MINUTES

8 cups (1.75 liters) water
2 lb (1 kg) beef chunks, cut into bite-size pieces
1 stalk lemongrass, smashed and cut into 3 pieces
2 tablespoons ginger, minced
6-8 garlic cloves
4 shallots
1 tablespoon salt
½ tablespoon ground coriander
2 tablespoons dark brown sugar or maple sugar (or
    Indonesian palm sugar)
½ teaspoon ground turmeric
2 cups (500ml) coconut milk
7 bay leaves
6 kaffir lime leaves or ½ teaspoon grated lime zest
2 potatoes, peeled and cut into small chunks

GARNISH
4 tablespoons coriander leaves (cilantro), roughly chopped
1 large tomato, cut into 8 wedges
4 tablespoons Fried Shallots (page 34)

Betawi Beef Soup   Soto Betawi

Forgotten by modern generations, the word "Betawi" is actually a version of the colonial name of present day Jakarta, once known to the Dutch as Batavia. Betawi refers to both the native people of Jakarta as well as this particular dialect of the Indonesian language. The Betawi people are an amalgamation of native Indonesian, Portuguese, Dutch, Chinese, and Arabs that have long been local inhabitants of this vast nation's capital. The soup named after them is no less a complex blend of ingredients, the result is a rich texture with full-bodied flavors. It has a smooth texture from the coconut milk but a hearty taste from the beef, which is why Betawi Beef Soup is so popular in Indonesia.

1 Bring the water to boil in a medium sized pot over high heat. Add the beef chunks along with the smashed lemongrass pieces and the ginger; simmer and stir occasionally.
2 Grind the garlic, shallots, salt, ground coriander, dark brown sugar , and turmeric using a mortar and pestle or food processor into a smooth paste. Spoon the paste into the boiling stock and stir until thoroughly combined. Lower the stove to medium high heat.
3 Pour in the coconut milk and toss in the bay leaves and kaffir lime leaves, stirring again until well mixed.
4 Carefully add the chopped potatoes and simmer for 20 to 25 minutes until the beef and potatoes are fork tender. Ladle into serving bowls and garnish with the chopped coriander leaves, tomato wedges, and Fried Shallots.

Chicken Chive Soup Sop Ayam Caisim

Whoever said that great food couldn't be healthy food obviously isn't familiar with Indonesian cuisine, or my grandmother. Her Chicken Chive Soup is incredibly easy and quick to prepare, resulting in a super light stock with a fragrance that can only be described as high-octane *umami*. Gently simmering chicken stock is the backdrop to a generous amount of garlic and ginger, infusing the soup with intense flavors. Lightly dredged in cornstarch, bites of chicken are briefly simmered, retaining their moisture and tenderness. My grandmother felt that chives were an underrated and underused vegetable in Indonesian cuisine, so she incorporated the onion-like greens along with crisp bamboo shoots to bring a flavorful balance to this charming soup.

SERVES 4
PREPARATION TIME: 15-20 MINUTES
COOKING TIME: 15-20 MINUTES

2 tablespoons oil
7-10 cloves garlic, finely minced
2 tablespoons minced ginger
8 cups (1.75 liters) chicken stock
2 small boneless, skinless chicken breasts, thinly sliced (1 lb/500 g)
2 tablespoons cornstarch
1 teaspoon salt + ¼ teaspoon for the chicken
1 bunch chives (4 oz/110 g), cut into 2-in (5-cm) long pieces
1¼ cups (150 g) fresh bamboo shoots (or canned)
⅛ teaspoon ground white pepper

1 Heat the oil in a large pot over high heat. Sauté the garlic and ginger until fragrant and lightly browned, for 1 to 2 minutes. Pour in the chicken stock and bring to a vigorous boil before lowering the heat to medium high.
2 Mix the chicken pieces with cornstarch and ¼ teaspoon salt with your hands until thoroughly coated.
3 Gently drop the chicken pieces into the stock and allow them to simmer for approximately 5 minutes.
4 Add the chives and bamboo shoots; stir gently. Toss in the remaining salt and the white pepper, continuing to stir. Simmer for another 3 minutes and serve hot.

SERVES 6-8
PREPARATION TIME: 15 MINUTES
COOKING TIME: 30 MINUTES

10 cups (2.25 liters) water

2 ears of corn, cut in half

12-16 cloves garlic

2 large shallots

¼ teaspoon ground red chili pepper

½ tablespoon dried shrimp paste (Indonesian *terasi* or Thai shrimp paste)

¾ cup (185 ml) tamarind concentrate

3 teaspoons salt

3 tablespoons sugar

⅓ head cabbage, roughly chopped to obtain 3 cups (150-200g)

5 oz (125 g) green beans, ends trimmed, cut in half

2-3 cups (250 g) eggplant, peeled and sliced in small chunks (any kind of eggplant)

½ lb (250 g) fresh shrimp, peeled with tails left on

Tamarind Vegetable Soup Jangan Asem

One of Indonesia's most famous soups, this Tamarind Vegetable Soup is a savory, tangy thirst quencher on hot days and pairs spectacularly with spicy seafoods or meats. Tamarind concentrates are now widely available in Asian markets all over the west, providing a perfect substitute for real, raw tamarind used in Indonesia. Uniquely piquant, with a taste that hits the back of the palate, the essence of tamarind really has no substitute. Tamarind lends a beautifully pulpy consistency and a rich, brown hue to this soup with its delicate balance of the sour, sweet, and salty.

1 Bring the water to a vigorous boil in a large pot over high heat. Add the corn and boil for 15 minutes.

2 Grind the garlic, shallots, ground red chili pepper, and shrimp paste using a mortar and pestle or food processor until a smooth paste is formed. Stir the paste into the boiling water, along with the tamarind concentrate, salt, and sugar.

3 Add the vegetables and shrimp into the soup, stirring thoroughly. Lower to medium high heat and simmer for 10 minutes. Ladle the soup into serving bowls and allow to cool for 10 to 15 minutes before serving. To enjoy the full flavor of this soup, serve it very warm instead of boiling hot.

Dutch-Indo Macaroni Soup

Sop Macaron

Here's a soup that can be found only in homes across Indonesia. Light and tasty, Dutch-Indo Macaroni Soup is another dish that finds its roots in Indonesia's Dutch influence. It takes a little bit of time to prepare but this soup can be kept for several days in the refrigerator and reheated without losing its subtle flavors. This is a fabulous alternative to the typical chicken noodle soup, particularly if you're craving a light meal.

SERVES 8
PREPARATION TIME: 15 MINUTES
COOKING TIME: 25-30 MINUTES

1 box elbow macaroni (8 oz/225 g)
10 cups (2.25 liters) chicken stock
½ lb (250 g) medium fresh shrimp, shell on and deveined
½ lb (250 g) ground or minced fresh boneless chicken meat
1 large egg
2 teaspoons salt + 3 teaspoons (for the soup)
¼ teaspoon white pepper
2 teaspoons cornstarch
8-10 button mushrooms, wiped and sliced thinly
1 medium carrot, diced
2 tablespoons butter
1 teaspoon sugar + 1 teaspoon for the soup

1 Bring a few inches (app. 8 cm) of water to a vigorous boil in a large pot and cook the macaroni until al dente, approximately 8 to 9 minutes. Drain the macaroni and set aside.
2 Bring the chicken stock to a boil in the same large pot after discarding the water used to make the macaroni.
3 Peel the shrimp and rinse under cold water. Grind the shrimp with the ground chicken, egg, salt, pepper, and sugar using a food processor until a smooth and thick paste forms. Remove the paste from the processor and place in a bowl. Add the cornstarch to the paste and mix with a spoon until thoroughly combined.
4 Once the chicken stock has come to a high boil, lower the heat to medium high. Drop small spoonfuls of the chicken shrimp mixture into the simmering stock. Once the spooned balls of chicken and shrimp are floating on the surface of the stock, simmer for another 3 to 5 minutes.
5 Slide in the mushrooms, carrot, macaroni, and butter. Toss in the remaining salt and sugar and stir the soup thoroughly, simmer for 5 minutes. Serve very warm.

Buckwheat Noodle Soup Misoa Kuah

There's something so incredibly comforting about noodles, particularly when they are in a warm soup. As a child I would get to indulge in this nutritious, delicious Buckwheat Noodle Soup whenever my mother wanted to prepare something quick and easy without sacrificing taste or nutrients. I could smell the sweet shrimp-infused stock and fragrant garlic emanating from the kitchen as I eagerly peeked from afar. The soft noodles in the delicate stock give such a warm swirl of mellow flavors, soothing away remnants of a bustling day. These thin, white noodles are amongst the most delicate of all noodles and are readily available in a dry, packaged form. The noodles beautifully capture the natural sweetness of the shrimp stock.

**SERVES 4   PREPARATION TIME: 10 MINUTES
COOKING TIME: 10-15 MINUTES**

10 cups (2.25 liters) water
½ lb (250 g) fresh medium shrimp, shelled
    with tails left on
7 oz (200 g) misoa noodles (somen) or rice
    stick noodles
20-30 cloves garlic, minced
½ large bitter melon, cut into small pieces
    (use cucumber or zucchini as a substitute)
2 teaspoons salt
1½ tablespoons sugar

1 Bring the water to a vigorous boil in a large pot over high heat.
2 Once the water has come to a boil, toss in the shrimp, simmering for just about 1 to 2 minutes.
3 Gently add the misoa noodles, simmering for another 4 to 5 minutes, stirring occasionally.
4 Combine the garlic, bitter melon, salt, and sugar, stirring thoroughly into the noodles. Turn off the heat and serve immediately.

Chicken Noodle Soup Soto Ayam

Few things speak to the human spirit more than a hearty bowl of Chicken Noodle Soup. It's unfortunate that with the extensive recipe sharing on the Internet, most people who've not been blessed with a visit to Indonesia still confuse "Laksa Ayam" for Soto Ayam. Laksa is a very similar to this Chicken Noodle Soup but it uses coconut milk as part of the stock, whereas Soto Ayam is a lighter, clearer stock with no coconut milk. These minor differences make the two soups vastly different in both taste and texture. Chicken Noodle Soup conjures wonderful memories of my childhood.

SERVES 4   PREPARATION TIME: 20-25 MINUTES
COOKING TIME: 30-45 MINUTES

4 cups (1 liter) water
6 cups (1.5 liters) chicken stock
3-4 chicken breasts or thighs, skinless, bone-in (2 lb/1 kg)
3 stalks lemongrass, tender inner part of bottom third only, bruised and cut into 3 parts each
16-18 cloves garlic
3 tablespoons ginger, minced
3 tablespoons galangal, minced
3 teaspoons ground coriander
½ teaspoon ground turmeric
2 teaspoons salt (if you are using unsalted chicken stock, add 1 more teaspoon of salt)
8 oz (250 g) dry cellophane noodles, soaked in warm water
2 tablespoons oil

GARNISHES
4 oz (100 g) bean sprouts, rinsed and drained
4 green onions (scallions), sliced into short lengths
4 large eggs, hardboiled
1 lime, cut into wedges
4 tablespoons Fried Shallots (page 34)
Coriander leaves (cilantro), chopped
Sambal oelek

1 Bring the water and chicken stock to a vigorous boil in a large pot over high heat. Once the soup has boiled for a couple of minutes, add the chicken and lemongrass, boiling for a few more minutes before reducing to medium heat. Simmer for at least ½ an hour, up to 45 minutes.
2 While the soup is simmering, grind the garlic, ginger, and galangal using a mortar and pestle or food processor, until they become a smooth paste. Over high heat in a small pan, sauté the paste in the oil for about 2 minutes until fragrant and it's just beginning to turn golden. Turn off the heat and add the ground turmeric. Sauté until well mixed. Set aside.
3 Once the soup has simmered for at least ½ an hour, transfer the chicken and lemongrass onto a plate. Stir the sautéed paste into the soup, along with the ground coriander and salt, stirring until the paste is thoroughly combined. Continue to simmer.
4 Using your hands or two forks, take the meat off the chicken bones and shred into thin slivers. Return the chicken meat to the simmering soup. Turn the heat back to high once again and allow the soup to come to a vigorous boil.
5 While the soup comes up to temperature, arrange the noodles in serving bowls. Place one hardboiled egg into each bowl. Turn the heat off and ladle the soup over the noodles and egg in the serving bowls. Garnish with fresh bean sprouts, chopped green onions, Fried Shallots, and coriander leaves. Serve with lime wedges and sambal oelek on the side.

Chapter Three
Salads

I love how Indonesian salads dispel any misconceptions about salads being boring. Indonesian salads are fearless in their combinations of fresh vegetables, fruits, seafood, and poultry— not to mention incredibly diverse in dressings. Tropical Fruit Salad with Palm Sugar Dressing (page 58) is a countrywide favorite; so much so that everybody from five star hotels to roadside stalls offers their unique versions of this sweet and sour salad. From the former Dutch influence, many Indonesian salad dressings have creamy textures and flavors, adding yet another dimension to the already vast array of ingredients found in Indonesia.

2 tablespoons oil
2 boneless, skinless chicken breasts
12 thin asparagus stalks (½ lb/250 g), ends
    trimmed
Bowl of ice water
4 romaine lettuce leaves, rinsed

TANGY SOY DRESSING
2 tablespoons soy sauce
6 tablespoons olive oil
1½ tablespoons Dijon mustard
1½ tablespoons balsamic vinegar
¼ teaspoon sugar
Freshly ground black pepper to taste

1 Heat the oil in a skillet over medium high heat.
Pan-fry the chicken breasts for approximately 5 to
7 minutes on each side until golden brown. Set the
chicken aside on a plate to cool down.
2 Bring 4 cups of water to a vigorous boil in a small
pot. While waiting for it to boil, cut the asparagus
into 2-inch pieces. Once the water has come to a
boil, turn off the heat and toss in the asparagus,
blanching for 30 seconds. Drain the asparagus
directly into the bowl of ice water, before draining
once again and placing it into a large serving bowl.
3 Tear up the romaine lettuce and toss together
with the asparagus pieces.
4 To make the Tangy Soy Dressing, whisk together
the soy sauce, olive oil, mustard, balsamic vinegar,
and sugar in a small bowl, until thoroughly combined and smooth. Set aside.
5 Cut the chicken into thin strips. Combine with the
lettuce and asparagus. Drizzle the Tangy Soy Dressing over the salad and add pepper to taste.

Chicken Asparagus Salad
Selada Ayam Asparagus

Like many Indonesian salads, Chicken Asparagus Salad is bright, flavorful, and incredibly easy to prepare. This dish is filled with essential proteins
and vitamins making it a healthy but light, summery dish. A nice twist to
this recipe is to use both green and white asparagus, which adds a rich color
palette and heartier texture. The soy sauce blends seamlessly with piquant
balsamic vinegar and mustard, dressing up these simple, fresh ingredients to
create a great salad for light fare.

Cellophane Noodle Salad Selada Soun

I'm not sure when it was exactly that my love affair with all things noodle began but I know it was very early on in life. My first memory of Cellophane Noodle Salad takes place at the Hyatt Hotel in Surabaya, Indonesia, where my family used to hold dinner parties with our extended relatives and friends. These parties most often took place by the hotel's beautiful swimming pool with an extensive BBQ buffet. Between games of tag and hide and seek, I would go back to the buffet for another serving of this light and fresh noodle salad, unable to resist its salty, zesty flavors. Cellophane noodles, also known as mung bean noodles or clear noodles, have the nutritional benefit of being lower in calories than most other noodles with no cholesterol. This salad's lively flavors, with its dash of sesame oil, create a savory yet light dish to be enjoyed by itself or as a side dish to grilled meats.

SERVES 4
PREPARATION TIME: 15-20 MINUTES + ½ HOUR SOAKING TIME
COOKING TIME: 2 MINUTES

One 7-oz (200-g) packet dry cellophane noodles
8-10 garlic cloves, finely minced
1 red onion, thinly sliced
8 kaffir lime leaves, finely cut or ½ teaspoon freshly grated lime zest
3 tablespoons coriander leaves (cilantro), roughly chopped
2 green onions (scallions), finely chopped
3 tablespoons finely chopped mint
2 tablespoons fresh lime juice
1 teaspoon sesame oil
1 teaspoon ground coriander
5 tablespoons soy sauce
½ teaspoon ground red chili pepper

1 Soak the cellophane noodles in a large bowl in warm water for at least ½ an hour and up to 2 hours.
2 Toss together the garlic, red onion, kaffir lime leaves, coriander leaves, green onions, and mint in a large mixing bowl.
3 Drain the soaked noodles. Bring about 5 to 6 cups of water to a vigorous boil in a medium sized pot. Boil the drained noodles for just about 1 to 2 minutes. Drain the noodles once again and toss in with the other ingredients in the large mixing bowl.
4 Add in the lime juice, sesame oil, ground coriander, soy sauce, and ground red chili peppers. Mix everything together until thoroughly combined. Serve warm or at room temperature.

Dutch-Indo Shrimp Salad Husaren Sla

The Dutch occupation of Indonesia introduced a number of unfamiliar flavors to the indigenous people that were quickly adopted into the local cuisine. This salad features some of these new flavors, with its rich, creamy dressing of butter, milk, and eggs. This vibrant salad has a beautiful combination of succulent shrimp, fresh vegetables, and juicy, tart pineapple chunks. The contrasting elements create luscious layers of sweet and savory flavors. With fresh ingredients, this salad can be presented in a dramatic tower of eye-popping colors, inviting people to feast with their eyes first. Indonesian salads typically incorporate salty and spicy elements but this Dutch-influenced extravaganza is more mellow in its flavoring.

SERVES 4-6
PREPARATION TIME: 30 MINUTES
COOKING TIME: 15-20 MINUTES

Water for boiling
2 potatoes, peeled and cubed (¾ lb/300 g)
2 medium carrots, peeled and diced (250 g)
¾ lb (350 g) fresh shrimp, shelled and deveined
3 large eggs, hardboiled, shelled, and sliced thinly
½ cup (250 g) fresh or canned pineapple chunks
½ large cucumber, diced (8 oz/250 g)
1 medium tomato, diced
Romaine lettuce to garnish

CREAMY DRESSING
3 tablespoons butter
3 tablespoons flour
1 cup (250 ml) whole milk
⅛ teaspoon salt + ½ teaspoon for the salad
1 teaspoon sugar
1 teaspoon white vinegar
¼ teaspoon ground nutmeg
Freshly ground black pepper to taste
1 large egg yolk

1 Fill a medium sized pot with a few cups of water and bring to a vigorous boil over high heat. Boil the potatoes and carrots for approximately 8 to 10 minutes until fork tender. Remove the potatoes and carrots from the pot and set aside to cool (do not throw out the hot water).

2 Blanche the shrimp in the same pot of boiling water for just about 1 minute until they turn a bright orange pink hue. Drain the shrimp and set aside to cool.

3 To make the Creamy Dressing, heat the butter in a small pot over medium high heat. Once the butter has melted, toss in the flour and stir vigorously until a smooth, thick paste is formed. Pour in the milk and use a whisk to continuously mix together with the butter-flour paste while adding the salt, sugar, vinegar, nutmeg, and pepper. Whisk rapidly over the heat for 3 to 5 minutes until the mixture reaches a smooth consistency.

4 Remove from the heat and add the egg yolk while whisking rapidly. Allow the Creamy Dressing to cool to room temperature.

5 While the dressing cools down, assemble the potatoes, carrots, shrimp, hardboiled eggs, pineapple chunks, cucumber, and tomato on a bed of lettuce on a large serving plate. Before serving, drizzle the Creamy Dressing over the salad.

Tangy Melon Salad Selada Buah Saus Mustard

Indonesians have mastered the fine art of creating the most addictive, luscious salads out of a variety of fresh fruits. Here, two vibrantly colored melons complement each other's flavors while a tangy dressing adds a surprisingly savory accent to an otherwise sweet dish. I love eating this Tangy Melon Salad on a hot summer day or anytime I'm craving fresh fruits. The mustard and white wine vinegar contrast beautifully with the sweet and juicy melons.

½ cantaloupe or rock melon (1 lb/500 g)
⅓ small watermelon (1 lb/500 g)

TANGY MUSTARD DRESSING
¼ teaspoon salt
Freshly ground black pepper to taste
⅛ teaspoon ground red chili pepper
1½ tablespoons sugar
1 teaspoon white wine vinegar
1 tablespoon Dijon mustard
5 tablespoons olive oil

SERVES 4   PREPARATION TIME: 15-20 MINUTES

1 Use a melon baller to extract little balls from both the cantaloupe and the watermelon. Do this step over a large mixing bowl, so both the melon balls and all their natural juices are captured in the bowl.

2 Whisk together the Tangy Mustard Dressing ingredients in a medium sized bowl until thoroughly combined and smooth. Drizzle this dressing over the melon balls and toss together gently until evenly coated. Refrigerate for 15 to 30 minutes before serving.

Salad á la Mama Selada Banjar

My first memory of eating Salad á la Mama was at a family reunion when I was about 12 years old. My parents' house was filled with the most enticing aromas of every herb and spice imaginable, but it was the crunching sounds of the thin potato chips that garnish this salad that lingered in my mind for weeks after I ate it. I've since introduced my family's recipe to countless friends and colleagues who have all fallen madly in love with its luscious, creamy dressing. Imagine cool, crisp lettuce with sweet tomato wedges, cucumber chunks, and a sprinkling of crunchy potatoes, all under a thick drizzling of the Sweet and Savory Dressing, coming together for one velvety, explosive bite.

**SERVES 4-6 PREPARATION TIME: 15-20 MINUTES
COOKING TIME: 10-15 MINUTES**

1 large potato, peeled
Oil for deep-frying
Salt for sprinkling
1 large cucumber, peeled and sliced
4 large eggs, hardboiled, shelled, and sliced thinly (for the salad)
1 head iceberg lettuce, sliced into bite-size chunks
2 tomatoes, sliced into thin rounds

SWEET AND SAVORY DRESSING
8 large eggs hardboiled and shelled (use 5 whole eggs and 3 just the yolks)
5 tablespoons mayonnaise
3 tablespoons Dijon mustard
2 tablespoons white vinegar
4 tablespoons sugar
¾ teaspoon paprika
¾ teaspoon salt
Freshly ground black pepper to taste

1 Slice the potato into extremely thin rounds; separate the slices on a non-stick baking pan and pat dry with a paper towel.
2 Heat the oil in a deep skillet or wok over medium high heat (when you pass your hands over the oil you should feel the heat strongly against your palms). Deep fry one handful of sliced potatoes at a time (be careful, splattering may occur); fry until golden brown and crisp. Drain on paper towels, patting any excess oil with another paper towel then sprinkle lightly with salt. Repeat this step until all the potatoes are fried, set aside.
3 Cut the cucumber lengthwise in half then into thin slices (half moon shapes) and set aside. Arrange the lettuce, cucumbers, tomatoes, and eggs on serving plates.
4 To make the Sweet and Savory Dressing, blend together 5 whole eggs plus 3 yolks, mayonnaise, mustard, vinegar, sugar, paprika, salt, and pepper in a food processor blending until smooth and creamy. Drizzle over the salad and top with crunchy potato slices. Serve immediately.

Mango and Grilled Shrimp Salad

Selada Mangga Udang Bakar

This dish perfectly represents the best features of Indonesian cuisine. Indonesia is famous for its many varieties of luscious mangos as well as an abundance of fresh, succulent seafood. Here, I offer a more convenient method of "grilling" the shrimp. If you have enough time and an outdoor grill, you can grill the shrimp the old fashioned way, which will yield a smoky flavor. Sweet mangos and juicy shrimp combine the gritty dark brown sugar, fragrant toasted coconut, and a dash of heat from the chili peppers.

SERVES 4
PREPARATION TIME: 20-25 MINUTES
COOKING TIME: 5 MINUTES

½ lb (250 g) fresh shrimp, shelled and deveined, tails on
1 teaspoon oil
¼ cup (125 g) green beans, ends trimmed and cut in half
Small bowl of ice water
3-4 ripe mangos (1½ lb/750 g), peeled, pitted and diced
¼ cup (125 g) red onion, thinly sliced
2½ teaspoons dark dark brown sugar
1 teaspoon sugar
¾ teaspoon salt
2 tablespoons coriander leaves (cilantro), finely chopped
2 tablespoons Fried Shallots (page 34)
2-3 bird's-eye chili peppers, finely chopped
¼ cup (15 g) toasted coconut flakes

1 Pre-heat the oven to high broil. Coat the shrimp with the olive oil, mixing thoroughly in a small bowl. Arrange the shrimp on a non-stick baking sheet and broil for 2 minutes on each side. Remove from the broiler and set aside to cool.

2 Bring approximately 2 cups of water in a small pot to a vigorous boil. Turn off the heat and toss in the green beans for just about 30 seconds. Drain the green beans and immediately plunge them into the bowl of ice water. Drain the green beans and place into a large bowl.

3 Add the rest of the ingredients along with the shrimp into the bowl with the green beans. Gently toss everything together until thoroughly combined. Serve immediately.

Tropical Fruit Salad with Palm Sugar Dressing Rujak

In the humid heat of Indonesia, keeping cool and hydrated can be a very tasty business. Found mostly in roadside stalls and traveling food carts, this fruit salad is a wonderful summertime treat. Not only is it packed with essential vitamins and nutrients, but also its intense flavors will leave an indelible mark on your palate. Some of the traditional fruits used in this fruit salad can only be found in Indonesia, so here in this recipe, I've substituted a few that can be found quite easily in the West. For the dressing though it's difficult to substitute for Javanese sugar, also known as *gula jawa*, if you can find it in your local Asian store or order it from an online source you'll get a more authentic Indonesian dish.

SERVES 4   PREPARATION TIME: 10-15 MINUTES

1 unripe green mango (½ lb/250 g) peeled, pitted and
    thinly sliced
1 green granny smith apple, cored and roughly chopped
    (120 g)
1 small ripe pineapple (1 lb/500 g), peeled, cored and cut
    into bite-size chunks
1 papaya medium ripe to ripe (1 lb/500 g), cut into bite-
    size chunks
3 water apples or 1 guava, washed and sliced

PALM SUGAR DRESSING
1 cup (200 g) dark brown sugar or maple sugar (or Indo-
    nesian palm sugar)
3 tablespoons water
1 teaspoon dried shrimp paste
1-2 red bird's-eye chili peppers
½ teaspoon salt
Juice of 1 lime

1 Toss together all the fruits in a large mixing bowl and set aside.
2 To make the Palm Sugar Dressing, blend the dark brown sugar, water, shrimp paste, chili peppers, salt, and lime juice in a food processor or blender until a smooth, thick consistency is achieved. Drizzle over the mixed fruits and toss together until thoroughly coated. Serve immediately.

Avocado and Smoked Salmon Salad Selada Avocado Saus Asam

Until I looked through my grandmother's collection of recipes, I never realized the extent of Indonesian cuisine's diversity. The memory and images I had of Indonesian food was one dimensional, focusing on the heavier flavors of shrimp paste, spices, and salt. This Avocado and Smoked Salmon Salad features the amazing taste of smoked salmon and a piquant dressing drizzled over the top. These ingredients may not sound like they are native to Indonesia, but because of foreign influences they have been integrated into Indonesia's everyday cuisine. Light, nutritious, and easy to prepare, this is an ideal dish for low calorie eating.

**SERVES 4   PREPARATION TIME: 20 MINUTES
COOKING TIME: 5 MINUTES**

1 head of arugula or romaine lettuce, washed and sliced
8 cherry tomatoes, halved
2 green onions (scallions), sliced
8 oz (250 g) smoked salmon
4 large eggs, hard boiled, and sliced
2 large ripe avocadoes, sliced

TANGY DRESSING
¾ teaspoon salt
4 tablespoons balsamic vinegar
¼ red onion, finely minced
¼ teaspoon ground red chili pepper
1½ tablespoons soy sauce
2 teaspoons sugar
6 tablespoons olive oil

1 Arrange the arugula or lettuce on serving plates with the tomatoes, green onions, and smoked salmon, placing the hardboiled egg slices and avocado slices on top.
2 To make the Tangy Dressing, whisk together the salt, balsamic vinegar, red onion, chili pepper, soy sauce, sugar, and olive oil in a mixing bowl until thoroughly combined. Drizzle evenly over the salads. Serve immediately.

Indonesian Mixed Salad with Creamy Peanut Dressing Gado Gado

Everybody's grandmother in Indonesia has a version of this Indonesian Mixed Salad with Creamy Peanut Dressing. I remember visiting senior citizens in countryside villages in Indonesia where I was invited to partake in family meals and they always included this peanut flavored salad. It's amazing how humble homes and bare-bone kitchens with no electricity can often produce the most mind-blowing foods. Tiny old ladies wearing batik sarongs with their waist-long hair piled in high buns, crouching on cement floors, using stone mortar and pestles to pound fresh roasted peanuts and chili peppers with energy and ferocity. I could only watch and learn as they expertly added spices and herbs, sautéed the coconut milk with the paste, and eventually tossed all types of greens, tofu, and bean sprouts in with the peanut sauce. Indonesians have an adept way of turning nutrient-rich ingredients into a dish that tastes sinfully good.

SERVES 4-6
PREPARATION TIME: 20-25 MINUTES
COOKING TIME: 15-25 MINUTES

Oil for deep-frying
½ head cabbage (1 lb/500 g) thinly sliced
3½ cups (375 g) bean sprouts
½ block firm tofu (8 oz/250 g)
1 large cucumber, peeled and sliced thinly
6 large eggs, hardboiled, shelled and sliced thinly
Shrimp chips for garnish

CREAMY PEANUT DRESSING
1 cup (100 g) raw peanuts
6-10 cloves garlic
2 stalks lemongrass, tender inner part of bottom third only, minced
½ tablespoon finely minced kaffir lime leaves or ¼ teaspoon finely grated lime zest
2 tablespoons oil
3 cups (750ml) coconut milk
½ teaspoon cayenne pepper
¾ teaspoon salt
3 teaspoons sugar

1 Heat the oil in a small wok or pot over high heat.
2 Bring a large pot of water to a vigorous boil. Turn off the heat once the water has come to boil. Blanch the chopped cabbage in the hot water for about 45 seconds to 1 minute until just soft. Remove, drain, and set aside the cabbage to cool. Repeat this blanching process with the bean sprouts, but leave them in the hot water

only for about 15 to 20 seconds. Set aside to cool as well.

3 Drain the tofu from its liquid and cut into small thin rectangles. Carefully slide the tofu pieces into the hot oil and deep fry for 3 to 5 minutes until crisp and golden brown. Drain on a paper towel.

4 Arrange the blanched cabbage, bean sprouts, cucumbers, and egg slices on a serving platter. Sprinkle the crisp tofu bits on top. Set aside.

5 Dry roast the peanuts over high heat in a wok or skillet, shaking the nuts around every few minutes. This process will take anywhere from 5 to 15 minutes depending on the heat of the stove. The peanuts should be a rich, dark brown color when done.

6 To make the Creamy Peanut Dressing, grind the roasted peanuts, garlic cloves, lemongrass, and kaffir lime leaves using a mortar and pestle or blend with a food processor until very smooth. Return the paste to the hot wok or skillet with the 2 tablespoons of oil and sauté for 2 to 3 minutes until fragrant and golden. Add the coconut milk, cayenne pepper, salt, and sugar, stirring until thoroughly mixed. Allow the mixture to come to a vigorous boil then immediately remove from the heat. Allow the peanut dressing to cool down, stirring occasionally as it cools.

7 Serve the salad with shrimp chips and the peanut dressing, either on the side or, for an authentic Indonesian presentation, toss the entire salad with the dressing before serving.

Cucumber Salad Selada Ketimun

Indonesians love having a variety of side dishes to accompany their main dish. Cucumber Salad is one of the most popular of those side dishes, although it's also often eaten as a small salad on its own. Fresh lime juice envelops the crunchy cucumber chunks in a refreshingly tart dressing, with zesty kaffir lime leaves providing an unforgettably aromatic accent. Sweet red onions and spicy chili peppers add different dimensions to this simple salad. Savory, sweet, and tangy cucumbers are an addictive accompaniment to many of Indonesia's spicy dishes. On a warm tropical day, when eating a grilled meat or curry with warm white rice, this Cucumber Salad helps to cool off a fiery meal.

2 large cucumbers (1 lb/500 g), cut into small chunks
1 red onion, thinly sliced
8 kaffir lime leaves, finely sliced
1-2 bird's-eye chili peppers, finely chopped
3 tablespoons fresh lime juice
¾ teaspoon salt
1½ teaspoons sugar

SERVES 4
PREPARATION TIME: 10 MINUTES

Toss all the ingredients together in a medium sized bowl until thoroughly combined. Allow the cucumber salad to sit for 10 minutes before serving. Store up to 3 days in a tightly sealed container.

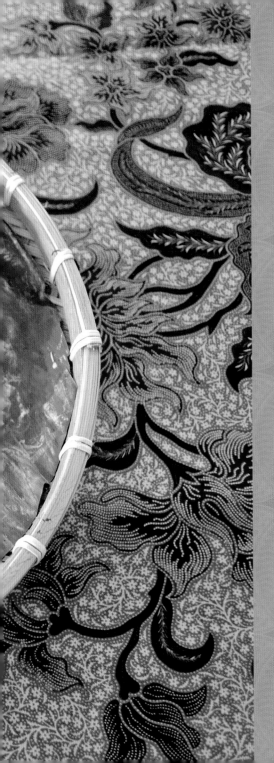

Chapter Four
Poultry and Meat Dishes

Different regions of Indonesia specialize in different ingredients and methods of cooking. Balinese Roast Chicken is first bathed in thick, sweet soy sauce and spicy chili paste before being slow roasted to produce an incredibly luscious and savory dish. In the western regions, rich curries play a major role in daily meals, with aromatic garlic and onion starring front and center. All meat and poultry dishes in Indonesia have one thing in common and that is their explosive and pungent flavors, unabashed in their attempts to tantalize anyone passing by.

SERVES 4-6
PREPARATION TIME: 10-15 MINUTES
COOKING TIME: 50-55 MINUTES

½ tablespoon ground red chili pepper

1 tablespoon dried shrimp paste (Indonesian *terasi* or Thai shrimp paste)

2 shallots, peeled and roughly chopped

15-20 cloves garlic

3 stalks lemongrass, tender inner part of bottom third only, finely minced

Two 2-inch (5-cm) pieces galangal, peeled and roughly chopped

2 tablespoons oil

1 fresh chicken, cut into 8 pieces (mix of drumsticks, thighs, wings, and breasts, bone-in)

2 cups (500 ml) coconut milk

2 potatoes, peeled and cut into chunks

1 teaspoon salt

2½ teaspoons ground coriander

½ teaspoon ground turmeric

10 kaffir lime leaves or 1 teaspoon finely grated lime zest

Curried Chicken Kare Ayam

Curried Chicken is one of Indonesia's most famous dishes, blending a variety of herbs and spices to create a savory and heartwarming dish. To extract the most intense flavors, it's imperative to use chicken with the bones in. The key to fantastic Curried Chicken is to be indulgent with the seasonings. After all, chicken, potatoes, and coconut milk are all mildly flavored to begin with, so they make a great canvas for a beautiful meal when all the right ingredients are simmered together. As a garlic lover, I use a lot of it in this dish without making it the focal point. This is an easy dish to prepare and will keep well in the refrigerator for several days.

1 Grind the ground red chili pepper, shrimp paste, shallots, garlic, lemongrass, and galangal using a mortar and pestle or food processor until a smooth paste is formed.

2 Heat the oil in a wok or pot over high heat. Sauté the paste for 1 to 2 minutes until fragrant. Carefully place the chicken and coconut milk on top of the paste, stirring gently until the paste is mixed into the liquid. Bring to a vigorous boil then lower the heat to medium.

3 Add the potatoes, salt, ground coriander, turmeric, and kaffir lime leaves. Stir until thoroughly mixed. Simmer for 40 to 45 minutes, stirring occasionally.

Banjar Chicken Steak Ayam Banjar

Long after colonial occupiers left their subjects as independent states, their influences continue to surface as part of everyday life in Indonesia. Banjar Chicken Steak is a succulent reminder of the colonial years. I had a long argument with my mother over this recipe, I couldn't believe that an Indonesian recipe could possibly include tomato ketchup. She was proven right though, since the Dutch introduced the condiment to Indonesia years ago. Banjarmasin, for which this steak is named, is a small town where my mother grew up on the island of Kalimantan, also known as Borneo. Many of Indonesia's most famous dishes have originated from this area, where long ago a great amalgamation of Chinese, Dutch, and Indonesians co-existed. One can only imagine the fabulous delicacies that were created between the three peoples.

SERVES 4
PREPARATION TIME: 7-10 MINUTES
COOKING TIME: 15 MINUTES

4 boneless, skinless chicken breasts (2 lb/1 kg)
2 teaspoons salt
1 teaspoon ground nutmeg
8 tablespoons butter (1 stick/125 g)
2 large onions, peeled and sliced into thick rings

STEAK SAUCE
1 cup (250 ml) tomato ketchup
¾ cup (185 ml) sweet soy sauce
½ teaspoon salt

1 Rinse the chicken breasts and pat dry with a paper towel. Season both sides evenly with salt and nutmeg. In a non-stick skillet, melt the butter over medium high heat. Pan-fry the chicken breasts in the butter for about 5 to 6 minutes on each side until golden brown.
2 While the chicken is cooking, in a separate small pot, place all the ingredients for the sauce on high heat and bring to a vigorous simmer while stirring. Immediately take off the heat. Set aside.
3 Once the chicken is done, immediately arrange on a serving plate. In the same skillet that the chicken was cooked in, sauté the onion rings on high heat in the remaining bits of butter from the chicken. If the skillet is too dry, simply add a few tablespoons of olive oil or butter. Allow the onion rings to caramelize for 1 minute or so on each side. Place onion rings on top of the chicken steaks. Glaze with the Steak Sauce and serve immediately.

Indonesian Fried Chicken

Ayam Goreng Terasi

SERVES 4
PREPARATION TIME: 5 MINUTES
COOKING TIME: 20-25 MINUTES

1 fresh chicken, cut into serving pieces
1 teaspoon salt
½ teaspoon ground turmeric
2 teaspoons ground coriander
Oil for deep-frying
10-14 cloves garlic
½ tablespoon Shrimp Paste Chili Sauce
   (page 23)
8 tablespoons butter (1 stick/125 g)

1 Rinse the chicken under cold water and place in a large mixing bowl. Dust the salt, turmeric, and ground coriander over the chicken evenly.
2 Heat the oil in a large wok over medium high heat. Once the oil has come up to temperature, deep-fry the chicken for 8 to 10 minutes on each side until golden brown. Drain on a plate and remove the remaining oil from the wok. Return the wok to the stove.
3 Using a mortar and pestle or food processor, grind the garlic and Shrimp Paste Chili Sauce until a smooth paste is formed.
4 In the same wok, melt the butter over medium high heat and sauté the paste until thoroughly mixed. Add the fried chicken to the shrimp paste chili butter and mix until well coated, tossing lightly for about 3 minutes. Serve immediately.

One of my favorite aspects of Indonesian cooking is its pungent, intoxicating aromas, like that of shrimp paste, or *terasi*, as it is known in Indonesia. I can't resist fried chicken, especially when it's done right: juicy on the inside, super crisp on the outside. Add lots of garlic and a smothering of shrimp paste and we've got one of the most robust dishes known to mankind. Typically eaten with a side of Shrimp Paste Chili Sauce (Sambal Terasi), this fried chicken is served in households all over Indonesia. Be aware that when cooking my favorite fried chicken, your house will conspicuously be filled with the decadent scent of buttery chicken and salty shrimp paste, possibly drawing passersby to request a taste.

SERVES 4   PREPARATION TIME: 10-15 MINUTES
COOKING TIME: 50-60 MINUTES

4 chicken leg quarters (drumstick with thigh attached)
15-20 garlic cloves
1 large shallot, peeled and left whole
One 2-inch (5-cm) piece fresh ginger, roughly chopped to make
    1½ tablespoons
1 tablespoon oil
2 tablespoons butter
1 tomato, diced
2 stalks lemongrass, tender inner part of bottom third only,
    finely minced
16 kaffir lime leaves or 1½ teaspoons of lime zest
4 tablespoons sambal oelek
7 tablespoons sweet soy sauce
1 teaspoon salt
1 lime, cut into wedges

1 Preheat oven to 375°F (190°C). Rinse the chicken quarters thoroughly and pat dry with a paper towel. In a Pyrex dish or large baking sheet fully lined with aluminum, place the chicken side by side, close together. Set aside.
2 Using a mortar and pestle or food processor, grind the garlic, shallots, and ginger until a smooth paste is formed. Heat the oil and butter in a small pan over high heat. Sauté the paste until it's fragrant. Add the diced tomatoes, lemongrass, lime leaves, chili paste, sweet soy sauce, and salt. Sauté for another 3 to 5 minutes over medium high heat.
3 Pour the sauce evenly over the four chicken quarters, making sure to coat the entire chicken. Also make sure that the lime leaves are tucked in between the chicken legs and not laying on top of the surface area of the chicken. (The last ten minutes in the oven will be under the broiler so this step is to ensure that you don't end up with any burnt leaves).
4 Place the chicken in the oven and bake at 375°F (190°C) for approximately 45 minutes. The chicken skin should be lightly browned and slightly crisp. After the 45 minutes, turn the oven to high broil and allow the chicken to sit under the broiler for just about 10 minutes to crisp the skin further. Serve with wedges of lime and hot jasmine rice.

Balinese Chicken Ayam Bumbu Bali

Bali is world famous for being a paradise island. With a completely different culture and atmosphere than the rest of Indonesia, Bali also has its unique brand of Indonesian cuisine. This grilled chicken dish is extremely popular around the country with its glaze of traditional Balinese sauce. This quintessential Balinese sauce has become so widely popular and well known that variations of Balinese Chicken have arisen, substituting pork, fish, and vegetables for the chicken. If you have a grill, then you can barbeque the chicken with the sauce as the Balinese do to get the original smoky flavors. This recipe can be used for either outdoor grills or oven roasting.

Butter Fried Chicken — Ayam Goreng Romboter

Different regions of Indonesia have unique versions of dishes. One delicacy that seems to be extremely popular is the Butter Fried Chicken. Around the world, this dish is incredibly common and viewed as nothing particularly special. In Indonesia though, the mastery of chicken preparation is at a completely different level. Versions of fried chicken range from the super crispy with thick skins á la KFC to the super savory with a light, airy and crumbly exterior. Butter Fried Chicken is one of my all time favorites, crisp and packed with luscious flavor.

SERVES 4
PREPARATION TIME: 12-15 MINUTES
COOKING TIME: 15-25 MINUTES

Oil for deep-frying
1 fresh chicken, cut into serving pieces
3 tablespoons garlic powder + 1 teaspoon for the butter
2 teaspoon salt + 1 teaspoon for the butter
1 teaspoon ground turmeric
1 teaspoon ground nutmeg
12 tablespoons butter (1½ sticks/175 g)

1 Heat enough oil for deep-frying in a large wok over medium high heat.
2 Rinse the chicken pieces thoroughly and place in a large mixing bowl. Sprinkle all the spices evenly over all the chicken, rubbing gently into the skin. Allow the chicken to sit for 10 minutes.
3 Deep-fry the chicken a few pieces at a time, as many as the wok will allow without overcrowding. Cook on each side for approximately 5 to 6 minutes. Larger pieces such as breasts may require longer cooking times. Drain the cooked pieces on paper towels before transferring to a serving plate.
4 Melt the butter in a small saucepan over high heat and stir in 1 teaspoon of garlic powder and 1 teaspoon of salt until thoroughly mixed. Drizzle the melted butter over the fried chicken just before serving.

Sweet and Spicy Shredded Chicken Ayam Orang Aring

I love dishes that are savory and sweet and easy to prepare. Sweet and Spicy Shredded Chicken tastes fantastic whether served hot or at room temperature as long as it's eaten with steamed white rice. This is a great dish to cook ahead of time and keep in a sealed container in the refrigerator for the following days. The pungency of shrimp paste blends well with the sweet and spicy accents, coating the moist pieces of chicken. A minimal amount of oil results in an intensely flavored dish without extra calories or fat.

SERVES 4
PREPARATION TIME: 10 MINUTES
COOKING TIME: 8-10 MINUTES

2 tablespoons oil
8 cloves garlic, finely minced
¼ large red onion, finely diced
2-4 bird's-eye chili peppers, sliced diagonally
1 tablespoon dried shrimp paste (Indonesian *terasi* or Thai shrimp paste
2 fresh, boneless, and skinless chicken breasts, sliced into thin strips
¼ cup (65 ml) water
2 tablespoons sweet soy sauce
1 tablespoon sambal oelek
¾ teaspoon salt

1 Heat the oil in a wok on high heat. Sauté the garlic, onion, chili peppers, and shrimp paste until fragrant and lightly browned.
2 Add the chicken and sauté for about 2 minutes until browned. Add the water and lower heat to medium high.
3 Add the sweet soy sauce, sambal oelek, and salt. Stir until thoroughly mixed for another 2 to 3 minutes. Serve with warm rice.

Carmelized Pork Babi Manis

Carmelized Pork is my grandmother's recipe from her young adult years going back and forth between China and Indonesia. This is a decadent dish, perfect for savoring slowly on a lazy day. Caramelized sugar and salty fish sauce blend to luxuriously coat the tender pork chunks, resulting in a rich, ooey gooey sauce that is simply divine shen served over white rice. Even though I feel like I should run a marathon every time after I eat this dish, I know each sinful bite was worth it. Though the steps may sound complicated, they're really quite simple once you begin cooking.

SERVES 4   PREPARATION TIME: 15-20 MINUTES
COOKING TIME: 45-55 MINUTES

¼ **red onion, thinly sliced**
1½ **cups (375 ml) warm water for soaking + ½ cup (125 ml) for marinade**
1½ **teaspoons salt**
Juice of ½ lime
¼ **teaspoon ground white pepper**
2 **tablespoons sambal oelek**
5 **tablespoons fish sauce**
2 **tablespoons sugar for marinade + 1 cup for cooking**
1¼ **lb (600 g) boneless pork ribs or loin, cut into large, bite-size pieces**
1 **cup (250 ml) cold water**

1 Soak the sliced onions in 1½ cups of warm water along with the salt in a large bowl. Toss thoroughly and allow to sit for about 3 minutes, then rinse the onions under cold water and drain.
2 Return the onions to the bowl, adding the remaining ½ cup of warm water, lime juice, white pepper, sambal oelek, fish sauce, 2 tablespoons of sugar, and the pork chunks. Mix until the pork is thoroughly coated and all the ingredients have dissolved.
3 Caramelize 1 cup of the sugar over medium high heat, starting with a cold wok or pot. The sugar should caramelize in 4 to 7 minutes depending on the heat used. Once the sugar begins to melt, gently shake the wok or pot to redistribute the sugar as evenly as possible.
4 Once the sugar has turned a beautiful golden caramel color, carefully add the marinated pork and onion mixture. Take care to protect yourself from any splattering caramel because if it hits bare skin it is very painful. Using a wooden spatula, stir the pork and caramel vigorously, making sure to scrape the bottom of the wok or pot. Parts of the caramel will harden when the pork mixture is added due to the difference in temperature. However, once the pork has come up to temperature, the caramel will begin to melt again.
5 Add the cup of cold water bit by bit, mixing it slowly into the simmering pork. Lower heat to medium and simmer for 30 to 40 minutes, stirring occasionally. The pork is done once the liquid has reduced to a thick, syrupy consistency. Serve immediately with steamed rice.

SERVES 4-6
PREPARATION TIME: 10 MINUTES
COOKING TIME: 15-20 MINUTES

2½ tablespoons oil
8-12 cloves garlic, finely minced
2 tablespoons finely minced fresh ginger,
½ teaspoon dry ground red chili pepper (optional)
¾ lb (350 g) ground pork
1 lb (500 g) firm tofu, drained and cubed
3 tablespoons soy sauce
½ teaspoon ground white pepper
1 teaspoon sugar
1 tablespoon cornstarch
½ cup (125 ml) cold water
1 teaspoon sesame oil
2 green onions (scallions), sliced

1 Heat the oil in a wok over high heat. Sauté the garlic, ginger, and ground red chili pepper (if using) until it is lightly browned and fragrant.

2 Add the pork and sauté another 2 minutes. Add the cubed tofu, gently stir-frying until well mixed. Lower the heat to medium high.

3 Add the soy sauce, white pepper, and sugar; simmer for about 5 minutes.

4 Mix the cornstarch with the water and add a few tablespoons to the tofu mixture. Sauté gently, making sure to lift and fold the tofu over instead of mashing it with the spatula. Turn off the heat, and add the sesame oil and green onions. Toss together and serve.

Indonesian Mapo Tofu Mun Tahu

I first learned to cook Mapo Tofu when I was 13 years old. On a sunny Saturday in Indonesia when my grandfather was supposed to be spending a quiet afternoon with me at home while my parents were out, he decided that we were going to eat at his favorite Chinese Indonesian restaurant in town, The Mandala Restaurant. Famous for its Chinese influenced Indonesian cuisine, it was a hole-in-the-wall eatery that only locals frequented. That afternoon, my grandfather taught me the subtleties of a great Indonesian Mapo Tofu. How the tofu should be silky soft, how the hint of heat from the chili pepper and white peppers should barely tingle the back of the palate and how just a touch of aromatic sesame oil was needed to round out the delicate flavors of the dish.

Coconut Beef Stew Rendang

Indonesians are adept at transforming what are typically thought of as heavy ingredients into dishes that are rich without being overwhelming. Indonesia's Coconut Beef Stew incorporates chunks of meat into thick coconut milk simmering with a variety of herbs and spices. A generous amount of garlic and citrusy lemongrass fuse to intensify the curry-like stew while chili paste and ginger create an addictive sense of heat. A moderate simmer results in exquisitely tender bites of beef that melt in your mouth. This is a beautiful dish for introducing people to Indonesian cuisine and is sure to create fans. Always served with a bed of hot white rice, the Coconut Beef Stew casts a tantalizing cascade of spicy, full-bodied coconut sauce over everything it touches.

SERVES 4
PREPARATION TIME: 7-10 MINUTES
COOKING TIME: 40-50 MINUTES

12-16 cloves garlic
2 in (5 cm) fresh ginger, peeled and sliced
1 in (2.5 cm) fresh galangal root, peeled and sliced
2 stalks lemongrass, tender inner part of bottom
   third only, finely minced
1½ lb (750 g) beef sirloin chuck (or any cut for
   short stewing time)
2 tablespoons oil
2 teaspoons sambal oelek
2 cups (500 ml) coconut milk
¾ teaspoon salt
1 teaspoon freshly ground black pepper, or to taste
½ teaspoon sugar
¼ teaspoon ground turmeric
10 kaffir lime leaves or 1 teaspoon lime zest

1 Using a mortar and pestle or food processor, grind the garlic, ginger, galangal, and lemongrass until they become a smooth paste. Set aside.
2 Cut the beef into bite-size chunks.
3 Heat the oil in a wok or medium sized pot over high heat. Sauté the paste along with the sambal oelek for 1 to 2 minutes until fragrant.
4 Add the beef chunks and stir-fry for just a minute until thoroughly mixed. Pour in the coconut milk, tossing in the salt, pepper, sugar, ground turmeric, and lime leaves. Stir well and bring the stew to a vigorous boil.
5 Lower to medium high heat and simmer uncovered for 30 to 40 minutes until the coconut milk has reduced. Make sure to stir thoroughly every 10 minutes or so to ensure that nothing sticks to the bottom of the wok or pot. Once the beef stew has thickened, serve immediately with steamed white rice.

Spicy Lemongrass Beef Daging Asam Pedas

SERVES 4
PREPARATION TIME: 10-12 MINUTES
COOKING TIME: 15-18 MINUTES

Whenever I'm going to prepare a meal for my maternal uncle I rifle through my collection of Indonesian beef recipes. As a traditional Asian man, he feels that he hasn't really eaten unless he's had a meal with beef and rice. Spicy Lemongrass Beef has everything my uncle loves: tender chunks of meat bathed in cooked tomatoes, citrusy lemongrass, and piquant tamarind. Adding little red chili peppers provides a spiciness that makes the white rice accompaniment to this dish a very welcome addition. Despite the complex layers and full-bodied flavors in this Spicy Lemongrass Beef, preparation and cooking time are minimal for a dish that can easily dazzle meat loving family and friends.

6 cups (1.5 liters) water

2 lb (1 kg) beef chuck or stewing beef, cut into bite-size chunks

12-16 cloves garlic

4 stalks lemongrass, tender inner part of bottom third only, finely minced

1-2 teaspoons ground red chili pepper

½ teaspoon ground cinnamon

½ teaspoon ground clove

6 tablespoons tamarind concentrate

3 tablespoons oil

2-3 medium tomatoes (1 lb/500 g), cut into small chunks

2 teaspoons salt

2 tablespoons sugar

10 kaffir lime leaves or 1 teaspoon lime zest

1 Bring the water to a vigorous boil in a medium sized pot over high heat. Add the beef and cook for 5 minutes. Drain the beef and set aside.

2 Using a mortar and pestle or food processor, grind the garlic, lemongrass, chili pepper, cinnamon, clove, and tamarind until a smooth paste is formed.

3 Heat the oil in a wok over high heat. Sauté the paste for 1 to 2 minutes until fragrant and lightly browned. Place the beef, tomato chunks, salt, sugar, and lime leaves into the wok. Stir until thoroughly mixed, bringing to a boil. Reduce to medium heat and simmer for 4 to 5 minutes, stirring occasionally. Serve hot with rice.

Chapter Five

Fish and Seafood Dishes

With more than 17,000 islands, Indonesia is the world's largest archipelago and it is no surprise that one of the main components of its cuisine is seafood. There are incredible flavors to be found in Indonesia's fish and seafood dishes, some exhibiting intense and spicy accents while others are mild, allowing the fresh ingredients to stand vibrantly alone. Grilled fish and calamari are easy and quick to prepare—light in flavor and use little to no oil. Dishes such as Shrimp with Spicy Bean Sauce elevate stir-fries to a new level of exquisite simplicity.

MAKES 1 WHOLE FISH   PREPARATION TIME: 15-20 MINUTES
COOKING TIME: 20-25 MINUTES

1 whole snapper or any firm textured fish (1½ lb/750 g)
Oil for deep-frying
2 tablespoons oil
12-16 cloves garlic
2 large shallots, sliced
2½ teaspoons salt
½ large tomato, diced
3 tablespoons sambal oelek
1 lime, sliced into wedges
1 small cucumber, to garnish.

1 Clean and scale the fish and rinse it under cold water. Pat dry with a paper towel and set it on a large plate. On each side of the fish, using a sharp knife, make approximately 2-inch long cuts between the top of the fish and its stomach area. Do this so there are 4 slits on each side. Set the fish aside.

2 Heat the oil for deep-frying in a large wok over medium high heat. Using a mortar and pestle or food processor, grind the garlic, shallots, and 1 teaspoon of salt until they become a smooth paste. Add the diced tomatoes. If using a mortar and pestle, gently mash the tomatoes into the garlic and shallot paste just a few times until lightly crushed. If using a food processor, pulse a few times.

3 Heat the 2 tablespoons of oil in a small pan over high heat. Sauté the paste for 1 to 2 minutes, adding the sambal oelek and remaining salt. Stir thoroughly for just a couple of minutes until fragrant and the tomatoes have dissolved further, creating a chunky sauce. Set the sauce aside.

4 Once the frying oil has come up to temperature, gently slide the whole fish in and deep fry for at least 7 to 8 minutes on each side, until completely golden and crisp. Drain thoroughly and arrange on a serving platter. Spread the sauce all over the fish. Garnish with lime wedges and cucumber pieces and serve hot.

Crispy Fish with Chili Sauce

Ikan Goreng Balado

Nothing showcases the brilliant simplicity of Indonesian cuisine than this luscious whole fish, fried to golden perfection and glazed with a chili sauce. This can be the centerpiece to any meal, great with hot white rice and an assortment of fresh vegetables and a side of Shrimp Paste Chili Sauce. With a little bit of effort and time, this dish can be made beautifully in a home kitchen. Always make sure to start with a fresh fish to ensure best results.

Sweet Soy Roasted Fish Ikan Bakar

There is something so deliciously alluring about the fresh scent of sea salt mingling with sweet soy sauce dripping from a grilled fish. All over Indonesia, from the capital city of Jakarta to the seaside villages in Bali, nondescript restaurants serve morning caught fish glazed in a simple mixture of sweet soy sauce and salt, grilled over an open flame. Besides the fact that this is a protein packed, low calorie dish, Sweet Soy Roasted Fish is a succulent staple in Indonesia, typically eaten with warm steamed rice and a side of spicy condiments and raw vegetables (known as *lalapan*). Whenever I miss that unmistakable Indonesian flavor, that finger licking caramelized goodness, I use this recipe, which is an easy alternative for home kitchens.

SERVES 4
PREPARATION TIME: 15-20 MINUTES
COOKING TIME: 25-30 MINUTES

1¾ lb (850 g) whole fish (any medium texture fish such as tilapia or pompano or trout)
1 cup (250 ml) sweet soy sauce
1 tablespoon fresh lime juice
1½ tablespoons sea salt
1 lime, cut into wedges
½ cucumber, sliced

1 Scale, clean, and ri nse the fish. Score the fish using a sharp knife three to four times on each side, making approximately two-inch slanted slices into the flesh.
2 In a large baking dish, pour the sweet soy sauce and lime juice over the fish and rub evenly all over both sides. Allow to sit and marinate for about ten minutes.
3 Preheat oven to 375°F (190°C). Sprinkle the salt evenly on both sides of the fish. Bake the fish for approximately 20 minutes.
4 Then turn the oven to high and broil fish for about 5 to 10 minutes depending on the strength of the oven. The top of the fish should be just beginning to caramelize and brown. Serve the fish immediately with lime wedges and cucumber slices on the side.

Grilled Swordfish with Fragrant Yellow Rice

Ikan Bakar Dengan Nasi Kuning

An idyllic afternoon I once spent in an Indonesian countryside resort entailed lounging in a wooden balé (wooden hut on stilts) on batik pillows. A warm breeze was blowing through it and there was a not-so-distant melodies of Javanese *gamelan* music wafting in the air. That afternoon was made more heavenly by the addition of a perfectly prepared meal—fresh, grilled swordfish with a squeeze of lime juice served next to a bed of vibrantly colored turmeric rice with accents of rich coconut. Few things are as decadent in life as lazing about a balé, eating fish that melts in your mouth while watching the sun sway against a mountainous backdrop of lush green tea bushes.

SERVES 4   PREPARATION TIME: 5 MINUTES
COOKING TIME: 25-30 MINUTES

3 cups (600 g) uncooked jasmine rice
1½ cups (375 ml) water
1½ cups (375 ml) coconut milk
1 teaspoon salt for the rice + ½ teaspoon for the fish
½ teaspoon ground turmeric
4 swordfish steaks (2 lb/1 kg total)
1½ tablespoons olive oil
Freshly ground black pepper to taste
1 lime, cut into wedges

1 Rinse the rice in cold water using the bowl of a rice cooker, and then drain. Pour in the water, coconut milk, salt, and turmeric. Mix thoroughly. Cook the rice following the machine's instructions.
2 Rinse the swordfish steaks under cold water and pat dry with a paper towel. Heat the oil in a non-stick skillet over medium high heat. Pan-fry the swordfish for 4 to 6 minutes on each side, depending on the thickness of the steak. Both sides should be a golden brown.
3 Transfer the fish onto serving plates and sprinkle evenly with the salt and freshly ground black pepper.
4 Using a plastic or wooden spatula, mix the yellow rice thoroughly once more before plating to ensure a beautiful, even yellow color. Serve the fish and rice with lime wedges.

Tamarind Glazed Fish Garang Asem Bandeng

One of Indonesia's greatest female chefs, fondly known by her many fans as Aunt Tanzil, owned a hole-in-the-wall restaurant high in the mountains in Indonesia. My parents would take us on a road trip up to her restaurant about once a year for several years in a row, traversing winding roads enveloped by lovely tea plantations and frangipani (plumeria) trees. Aunt Tanzil was famous for many of her Indonesian dishes, one of which was a Tamarind Glazed Fish. With the natural, cool mountain breeze drifting through her open-air restaurant, we would feast on this lightly browned fish glazed with the intoxicating combination of tangy tamarind, fresh tomatoes, and zesty kaffir lime leaves. This is my mother's version of this savory and irresistible dish.

SERVES 4   PREPARATION TIME: 5 MINUTES
COOKING TIME: 25-35 MINUTES

3 tablespoons butter for sauce + 2 tablespoons for fish
½ large tomato, diced
10 kaffir lime leaves or 1 teaspoon finely grated lime zest
½ cup (125 ml) tamarind concentrate
¾ teaspoon salt + extra for sprinkling
3 tablespoons dark brown sugar
Freshly ground black pepper to taste
2 lb (1 kg) sea bass fillets

1 Heat the 3 tablespoons of butter in a small saucepan over high heat until completely melted and it begins to bubble. Sauté the diced tomato with the kaffir lime leaves for 1 to 2 minutes.
2 Add the tamarind concentrate, salt, sugar, and pepper, reducing the heat to medium low. Simmer for 6 to 8 minutes while stirring continuously; making sure to scrape the bottom of the pot so nothing gets burnt. The tomato should break down while the sauce thickens. Turn off the heat and set the sauce aside.
3 Heat the remaining butter in a large non-stick skillet over medium heat. Pan-fry the sea bass for about 8 to 10 minutes on each side, depending on the thickness of the fish.
4 Spoon the sauce onto a serving plate. Gently lay the fish on top of the sauce. Sprinkle lightly with salt and serve immediately. Alternately, drizzle the sauce on top of the fish.

Tamarind Roasted Shrimp   Asem Udang Bakar

One of the best aspects of Indonesian cooking is the grilled seafood. Natural wood or charcoal grilling isn't always feasible in home kitchens of course, so we find ways of getting around our lack of a grill by using a broiler and still manage to recreate savory delicacies like these Tamarind Roasted Shrimp. If you do happen to have a grill, put it to good use with this easy recipe and turn this dish into its authentic form with that unmistakable smoky essence. Tamarind has an intensely piquant flavor, but unlike lime or lemon, it has an underlying sweetness to it. Succulent shrimp dressed with thick tamarind concentrate, lightly broiled make for a super easy and quick dish. Salty and tangy, Tamarind Roasted Shrimp give the illusion of feasting on fresh seafood on an Indonesian beach with the scent of rolling ocean waves crashing nearby.

SERVES 4
PREPARATION TIME: 5 MINUTES + ½ HOUR MARINATING TIME
COOKING TIME: 6 MINUTES

16 large fresh shrimp, shelled, tail left on
5-7 cloves garlic, finely minced
½ cup tamarind concentrate
3 tablespoons soy sauce
1½ tablespoons sugar
4 tablespoons butter

1 Mix all the ingredients, except the butter, in a medium sized bowl until thoroughly combined. Allow the shrimp to marinate for ½ an hour in the mixture or overnight.
2 Pre-heat the oven to high broil.
3 Arrange the shrimp on a non-stick baking sheet. Divide the butter equally between the shrimp, placing a small dollop on each.
4 Broil the shrimp for approximately 3 minutes on each side until pink. Serve warm.

Shrimp with Spicy Bean Sauce Udang Sambal Taoco

Ground bean sauce has a very particular and pungent aroma, lending a full-bodied saltiness and rich brown color to dishes. Fresh shrimp quickly stir-fried with spices and a bean sauce will liven up a meal with little effort or time. Bean sauce is readily available in Asian grocery stores, usually found in the same aisle as soy sauce. It's thick and rich, making it a powerful ingredient, so a little goes a long way. Though this dish is finger-licking delicious, it does have a strong flavor. I would recommend this to those already familiar with Indonesia's bold culinary textures and tastes.

SERVES 4
PREPARATION TIME: 5-10 MINUTES
COOKING TIME: 5-8 MINUTES

1½ lb (750 g) fresh medium-sized
    shrimp, shells on
3 tablespoons oil
7-9 cloves garlic, minced
3 tablespoons ground black bean sauce
1½ tablespoons sambal oelek
½ tablespoon sweet soy sauce
4 tablespoons water

1 Using a sharp knife, cut a deep slit along the center of the back of the shrimp to create a butterfly effect. Remove any veins and rinse the shrimp under cold water. Set the shrimp aside.
2 Heat the oil in a wok or large pan over high heat. Sauté the garlic until golden and fragrant for about 1 to 2 minutes.
3 Toss in the shrimp, bean sauce, sambal oelek, sweet soy sauce, and water. Stir-fry thoroughly for 1 to 2 minutes. Once the shrimp have turned a bright pink-orange color, remove from the heat and serve immediately.

SERVES 4
PREPARATION TIME: 15-20 MINUTES
COOKING TIME: 5-7 MINUTES

1½ lb (750 g) medium fresh shrimp shelled and deveined, tails left on

2 tablespoons oil

1 tablespoon unsalted butter

10-14 cloves of garlic, minced

2 heaping tablespoons tomato paste

10 kaffir lime lives (substitute 1 heaping teaspoon of grated lime zest)

½ large tomato, diced

½ cup (125ml) water

2 tablespoons soy sauce

1 teaspoon paprika

1 heaping cup of dark brown sugar or maple sugar (or Indonesian palm sugar)

1 tablespoon fresh lime juice

½ teaspoon salt

¾ teaspoon freshly ground black pepper

Javanese Sugar Shrimp Udang Gula Jawa

Javanese sugar, or *gula jawa*, is a very distinct, dark brownish-red packed sugar that usually comes in cylindrical blocks. It is not the same as the typical palm sugars found in western markets that are light brown or tan in color. For this recipe you can substitute dark brown sugar if you really can't find Javanese sugar, though the flavors will differ to quite an extent. If you don't have a complete Asian grocery story in your area, it is well worth it to purchase it from an online store as you can store this sugar in a zip-lock bag in the refrigerator indefinitely. Succulent shrimp glazed with this unforgettable thick sweetness and the bright accents of lime leaves will have your family or guests begging for the recipe.

1 Rinse the shrimp under cold water and drain.

2 Heat the oil and butter in a wok over high heat. Sauté the garlic for 1 to 2 minutes until it becomes a golden brown and fragrant.

3 Combine the tomato paste and kaffir lime leaves or lime zest into the garlic; stir until the paste is dissolved.

4 Toss in the shrimp and add the tomatoes, water, soy sauce, paprika, dark brown sugar, lime juice, salt, and pepper. Sauté for just another minute until shrimp has turns a bright orange pink color. Garnish with shredded kaffir lime leaves.

Crispy Sweet 'n Spicy Calamari

Sotong Bumbu Bali

SERVES 4
PREPARATION TIME: 5 MINUTES
COOKING TIME: 30-40 MINUTES

I've had the great pleasure of eating this scrumptious delicacy in several off-the-beaten-path restaurants in Jakarta and Bali. For the longest time I could not figure out how they got the calamari so crunchy, especially when dressed in this thick, sweet, and spicy sauce. Fortunately, one of the chefs gave in to my persistent questions and here's the secret—it's done by boiling and deep-frying the squid twice, two times for both steps. This dish does take a little time to make, but is quite simple and more than worth the effort.

2 lb (1 kg) fresh small squid bodies, sliced into rings
1 tablespoon oil +more for deep frying
Salt for sprinkling
2 tablespoons sweet soy sauce
1 tablespoon sambal oelek

1 Bring a few inches (5-7 cm) of water to a vigorous boil in a medium sized pot over high heat. Once the water has come to a boil, gently slide the calamari into the water. Simmer for 5 minutes and drain. Repeat this step once more. Drain the rings and pat dry with a paper towel.
2 Heat oil for deep-frying in a wok over medium high heat. Deep-fry the calamari rings for 10 or so minutes until golden brown. You may have to do this step in two halves to ensure enough space for the rings to float around. Drain the rings on a plate lined with paper towels and allow to cool for a few minutes.
3 Now repeat step 2 again (without having to reheat the oil), deep-frying the calamari for another 10 or so minutes. This time the calamari should come out a little more golden and after leaving to cool again on the paper towel, it should be perfectly crunchy.
4 Heat the remaining tablespoon of oil in another small wok or skillet over high heat. Sauté the sweet soy sauce and sambal oelek for a few seconds until thoroughly mixed before tossing in the calamari rings. Mix the calamari and sauce before transferring to a serving plate. Sprinkle with salt and serve immediately.

Spicy Sautéed Calamari Sambal Cumi

SERVES 4
PREPARATION TIME: 10-15 MINUTES
COOKING TIME: 6-8 MINUTES

Spicy Sautéed Calamari is my favorite dish to make for friends who claim they don't like calamari. My experience has been that people think they don't like calamari because they've had the experience of eating overcooked calamari that feels like chewing on rubber bands. This Balinese dish however, boasts the quintessential flavors of Indonesia's paradise island, coating lightly sautéed calamari with fragrant garlic, sweet soy sauce, and tangy, spicy chili. Preparing Spicy Sautéed Calamari is so quick and easy, you can save your energy for making more after friends and family inevitably change their minds about this tender seafood delicacy. One taste of this sweet and spicy dish will have the most finicky eaters becoming ardent calamari fans.

1 lb (500 g) calamari, bodies only
12 garlic cloves
1 large shallot, sliced
1 small onion (yellow or white), sliced
3 tablespoons oil
1 tablespoon butter
2 tablespoons sambal oelek
2 tablespoons tamarind concentrate
2 tablespoons sugar
¾ teaspoon salt
¼ teaspoon ground coriander
¼ cup (65ml) water
2 tablespoons chopped coriander leaves (cilantro), to garnish

1 Clean the calamari, rinsing thoroughly. Slice the calamari into small rings and set aside.
2 Using a mortar and pestle or food processor, grind the garlic, shallot, and onion until they become a smooth paste.
3 Heat the oil and butter in a wok or large skillet over high heat. Sauté the paste in the oil and butter until fragrant and translucent, about 1 to 2 minutes. Add the sambal oelek, tamarind, and sugar. Stir for another minute until everything is well blended. Add the calamari, salt, ground coriander, and water. Sauté for another 1 to 2 minutes until the coriander has shrunk slightly and serve immediately. Garnish with chopped coriander leaves.

Sweet Grilled Calamari Sotong Bakar

Having had the blessing to live in Indonesia as something of an upscale beach bum, I discovered one of life's most decadent pastimes. What could be more indulgent than laying around on a pristine, white sand beach with absolutely nothing around except the gently lapping waves of the azure Java Sea beckoning? Add to that image the sight of just-caught seafood being grilled right before your very eyes. Small, whole squids are first marinated in a simple bath of Indonesia's favorite sauce: sweet soy sauce. Then lightly sprinkled with salt before hitting a flaming grill. Barely a minute on either side renders the calamari super tender with finger-licking good caramelization.

SERVES 4
PREPARATION TIME: 5 MINUTES + ½ HOUR MARINATING TIME
COOKING TIME: 8 MINUTES

1 lb (500 g) baby calamari tubes, no tentacles
2 tablespoons sweet soy sauce
Salt for sprinkling

1 Clean the calamari tubes thoroughly, rinsing well under cold water. Pour the sweet soy sauce over the calamari in a medium sized bowl. Marinate for at least ½ an hour, or up to overnight.
2 Pre-heat oven to high broil.
3 Line a baking sheet with aluminum foil. Place the calamari tubes side by side on the sheet. Broil for 5 to 6 minutes on the first side and 3 minutes on the second side.
4 Remove from the broiler and sprinkle lightly with salt. Serve immediately.

Chapter Six

Rice and Noodle Dishes

Many of Indonesia's world famous dishes are right here in this chapter including all-time favorites such as Classic Nasi Goreng (page 89) and Rice Noodles with Meatballs (page 95). From savory stir-fries to spicy noodle soups laden with garlic, Indonesia's rice and noodle dishes are highly addictive comfort foods. In addition to the international favorites, I've also included some lesser-known dishes that are commonly eaten in family homes around Indonesia, such as Fragrant Garlic Rice Stew (page 91).

Traditional Coconut Rice Platter Nasi Lemak

Nasi Lemak is one of the most popular of Indonesian dishes, finding its way from casual street stalls to five-star hotels. There are many variations on this rich and full dish; here, I offer accompanying side dishes to the fragrant coconut rice that are savory and spicy without some of the heavier curries others like to use. Creamy coconut milk lends a smooth, sweet flavor to regular rice while side dishes of traditional fried chicken; spicy, salted anchovies; and fresh, cold cucumbers add a balanced contrast. Despite what seems like quite a few steps, Traditional Coconut Rice Platter is not very difficult to prepare and, with a lovely presentation, it can be an impressive dish to serve guests.

2 cups (400 g) uncooked rice
2½ cups (625 ml) water
¾ cup (185 ml) coconut milk
½ teaspoon salt for the rice + ¾ teaspoon for the chicken
4 chicken thighs (bone in and skin on)
¼ teaspoon ground turmeric
½ teaspoon garlic powder
¼ teaspoon freshly ground pepper
1½ tablespoons oil + for deep frying
1 cup (30 g) dried salted baby anchovies
1 tablespoon sambal oelek
1 tablespoon sweet soy sauce
1 large cucumber

CONDIMENTS
Shrimp Paste Chili Sauce or sambal oelek
Shrimp chips

SERVES 4
PREPARATION TIME: 10-15 MINUTES
COOKING TIME: 25-35 MINUTES

1 Rinse the uncooked rice under cold water using the container of a rice cooker, and carefully drain. Add the water, coconut milk, and ½ teaspoon of salt, stirring the mixture thoroughly before returning to the rice cooker. Follow instructions for the rice cooker and let the rice cook accordingly.
2 Rinse the chicken under cold water in a medium sized bowl and drain them thoroughly. Sprinkle the ¾ teaspoon salt, turmeric, garlic, and pepper evenly over the chicken, rubbing lightly and tossing as necessary to coat. Allow the chicken to marinate for a few minutes.
3 Heat enough oil to deep-fry the chicken in a wok or large pot over medium high heat. Once the oil has come up to heat, gently slide the chicken into the oil with the skin side down and fry it, frying

Traditional Coconut Rice Platter

for 9 to 12 minutes until golden brown. Turn the chicken over and continue frying for another 10 to 12 minutes. Drain on a plate lined with paper towels before placing one piece each on 4 serving plates.
4 Heat the 1½ tablespoons of oil over medium high heat in a small pan. Toss in the salted baby anchovies and stir-fry for just a minute until very lightly browned. Spoon in the sambal oelek and sweet soy sauce, continuing to stir-fry for another 30 seconds or until the anchovies and the sauces have mixed thoroughly. Divide the anchovies

Classic Nasi Goreng Indonesian Fried Rice

Every Asian country seems to have its version of fried rice and Indonesia has its own signature dish. I can't think of another dish that is more widely eaten in the country or better known by tourists. What I love about Indonesia's version is its depth of flavors; it's salty and sweet rather than other, more bland interpretations. A substantial meal in itself, Classic Nasi Goreng is savory and hearty, making it a simple but addictive dish. Here, I'm providing an easy and traditional recipe that can be combined with any of your favorite meat or seafood, to create a sumptuous all-in-one meal.

evenly between the four serving plates, near the chicken.
5 Cut the cold cucumber in half, then into thin sticks. Divide evenly and arrange the cucumber on the serving plates.
6 Place the coconut rice alongside the chicken, anchovies, and cucumber. Serve warm.

SERVES 4   PREPARATION TIME: 5-10 MINUTES
COOKING TIME: 6-8 MINUTES

2 tablespoons oil
8 cloves garlic, minced
1 large shallot, minced
2 large eggs
4 heaping cups (700 g) cooked rice
2 green onions (scallions), roughly chopped
3 tablespoons soy sauce
2 tablespoons sweet soy sauce
½ teaspoon salt
¼ teaspoon ground turmeric
½ teaspoon ground coriander

GARNISHES
1 large cucumber, thinly sliced
1 tomato (8 oz/250 g), sliced

1 Heat the oil in a large wok over high heat, sauté the garlic and shallot until golden brown and fragrant.
2 Crack the eggs into the wok and scramble quickly until just cooked. Lower the heat to medium high.
3 Add the cooked rice, green onions, soy sauce, sweet soy sauce, and all the dry spices. Stir-fry until thoroughly mixed for about 2 to 3 minutes, making sure to scrape the bottom of the wok so that none of the rice gets burnt. Serve very warm.

4 quarts (4.5 liters) water
2 large chicken breasts, bone-in (3 medium
    chicken breasts) (1 lb/450 g)
3 cups (500 g) cooked rice
6-10 garlic cloves smashed
1½ teaspoons salt

GARNISH
1 green onion (scallion), thinly sliced
4 tablespoons Fried Garlic (page 27)
2 or 3 shrimp crackers

CONDIMENTS
Sweet soy sauce
Sriracha chili sauce

1 Vigorously boil the 3 quarts (3 liters) of water in a large pot or wok over high heat. Carefully slip the chicken into the boiling water and lower to medium high heat and boil the chicken for 40 minutes. Then remove the chicken and set aside to cool.
2 Spoon the cooked rice into the stock; stir and let it simmer over medium heat for 30 minutes, stirring occasionally.
3 While the rice is simmering in the stock, chop the cooled chicken into thin slivers and return to the stock; add the smashed garlic and salt.
4 Add the remaining 1½ quarts (1.5 liters) of water and simmer for another 30 minutes stirring occasionally. Once the porridge has reached a thick and smooth consistency, ladle the porridge into serving bowls. Sprinkle the green onion, Fried Garlic, and shrimp crackers over the porridge and serve with the sweet soy sauce and Sriracha chili sauce on the side.

Chicken Rice Porridge Bubur Ayam

In a country that has an amazing array of delicious food, it's difficult to determine what is the national favorite. However, my personal guess as to Indonesia's national favorite would have to be the Chicken Rice Porridge. Though it's classified as a type of soup, Indonesians eat this porridge throughout the day. It is so popular that several major hotels around the country dedicate midnight buffets to it. There are also a number of 24-hour hole-in-the-wall joints that specialize in making various versions of this popular porridge. During my college years, I would often visit Indonesia with friends, going on midnight runs to the local Bubur joint to satisfy those late night cravings. There's nothing like a steaming bowl of Chicken Rice Porridge with a heavy sprinkling of green onions (scallions) and fried garlic, generously drizzled with Sriracha sauce to bring a close a long day.

Fragrant Garlic Rice Stew Nasi Bakmoy

I make no excuses about adoring garlic and this Fragrant Garlic Rice Stew brings out the best in the pungent ingredient. Don't be intimidated by the long list of ingredients here; this recipe is actually fairly easy to make and doesn't take too much time as long as you keep organized. Indonesians love eating their rice with a soup dish, typically spooning the soup or stew over the rice. This recipe is both for meat and seafood lovers as it incorporates sweet pork, chicken, and shrimp all together. Lightly frying the garlic before combining it into the soup creates a deliciously fragrant and strong accent.

6 cups (1.5 liters) chicken stock

4 cups (1 liter) water

1 lb (500 g) pork loin, cubed

2 boneless, skinless chicken breasts, cubed

1 teaspoon salt for soup + ¼ teaspoon for the
shrimp mixture

1 tablespoon sugar

1 tablespoon sweet soy sauce

Freshly ground black pepper to taste

½ lb (250 g) fresh medium shrimp, peeled and
deveined

1 large egg

2 tablespoons cornstarch

2 tablespoons oil + more for deep frying

6-10 cloves garlic, minced

6 cups (1 kg) freshly cooked rice

4 tablespoons chopped coriander leaves
(cilantro) or parsley, to garnish

SERVES 4
PREPARATION TIME: 20 MINUTES
COOKING TIME: 20-25 MINUTES

1 Vigorously boil the chicken stock and water in a large pot over high heat. Add the pork and chicken, along with 1 teaspoon of salt and the sugar, sweet soy sauce, and pepper. Boil for 5 minutes, stirring occasionally, then reduce the heat to low.

2 Heat several inches of oil in a wok or a deep frying pan over medium high heat.

3 Using a food processor, purée the shrimp, ¼ teaspoon of salt, egg, and cornstarch until a smooth paste is formed. Using two small spoons, take dollops of the shrimp mixture, moving it back and forth between the spoons to create an oblong ball. Gently drop the shaped mixture into the hot oil. Repeat this step until you have as many shrimp balls that the wok or frying pan can hold without crowding them too much. You will have to work quickly here so the shrimp balls don't burn. Deep fry the shrimp balls for just 1 to 2 minutes on each side until lightly golden. Drain the shrimp balls on paper towels and set aside to cool briefly. If you still have any shrimp mixture remaining, simply repeat this step until you have used all of it.

4 Heat the remaining 2 tablespoons of oil in a small pan over high heat. Carefully add the minced garlic and sauté for 3 to 4 minutes until it becomes a deep golden brown. Remove from the heat and immediately slip the garlic (and any remaining oil) into the simmering soup.

5 Gently toss the shrimp balls into the soup, and stir well. Ladle the soup into individual bowls and serve each one with a plate of steaming white rice. Garnish with chopped coriander leaves or parsley.

Coconut Noodle Soup Nyonya Laksa

This Coconut Noodle Soup is nearly identical to Chicken Noodle Soup with the exception of two very important ingredients—coconut milk and rice noodles. While regular Chicken Noodle Soup is comforting and savory, Coconut Noodle Soup is full-bodied and creamy. Using rice noodles instead of cellophane noodles changes the texture of this soup from light and slippery to a more starchy and substantial bite. The fragrant coconut milk adds a new dimension, blending with all the ingredients to create a rich and succulent stock.

SERVES 4
PREPARATION TIME: 10-15 MINUTES +
½ HOUR SOAKING TIME
COOKING TIME: 40-45 MINUTES

2 cups (500 ml) water
6 cups (1.5 liters) chicken stock
4 chicken breasts or thighs, skinless, bone-in (2¾ lb/ 1.35 kg) or 1½ lb (750 g) fresh shrimp, shelled and deveined
3 stalks lemongrass, tender inner part of bottom third only, bruised
15-20 cloves garlic
Approx 3 large pieces fresh ginger, peeled and sliced
Approx 3 large pieces fresh galangal, peeled and sliced
2 tablespoons oil
½ teaspoon ground turmeric
2 cups (500 ml) coconut milk
3 teaspoons ground coriander
2 teaspoons salt (if using unsalted chicken stock, add 1 more teaspoon of salt)
8 oz (250 g) dried rice vermicelli-noodles, soaked in warm water for ½ hour , drained
4 hardboiled eggs, shelled and sliced

GARNISHES
½ cup (50 g) bean sprouts, rinsed and drained
4 green onions (scallions), cut into small diagonal pieces
1 lime, cut into wedges
4 tablespoons Fried Shallots (page 34)
4 tablespoons chopped coriander leaves (cilantro)
Sriracha chili sauce (optional)

1 Bring the water and chicken stock to a vigorous boil in a large pot over high heat. Add the chicken and lemongrass. Once the soup has boiled for a couple of minutes, reduce to medium heat and allow the soup to simmer for at least ½ an hour, up to 45 minutes.

2 While the soup is simmering, using a mortar and pestle or food processor, grind the garlic, ginger, and galangal until they become a smooth paste. Heat the oil in a small pan over high heat, and; sauté the paste for about 2 minutes until it becomes fragrant and just begins to brown. Turn off the heat and add the ground turmeric. Sauté until well mixed. Set aside.

3 Once the soup has simmered for at least ½ an hour, remove the chicken and set aside. Spoon the sautéed paste into the soup, along with the coconut milk, ground coriander, and salt, stirring thoroughly. Continue to simmer.

4 Using your hands or two forks, take the chicken meat off the bones and shred into thin slivers. Return the chicken to the simmering soup. Turn the heat to high again and allow the soup to come to a vigorous boil again.

5 While the soup comes up to temperature, arrange the drained noodles in serving bowls. Place one egg in each bowl. Turn the heat off and ladle the soup over the noodles in the serving bowls. Garnish with fresh bean sprouts, chopped green onions, lime, Fried Shallots, and coriander leaves. Serve very warm.

Stir-fried Rice Vermicelli Bihun Goreng

Stir-fried Rice Vermicelli may seem identical to Stir-fry Noodles with Shrimp but in fact, has a very different flavor and texture. This has been one of my all time favorite noodle dishes since childhood. A classic Indonesian dish, Stir-fried Rice Vermicelli features thin rice stick noodles and is lighter than most other noodle dishes that use egg noodles. My version uses only vegetables, but you can add any meat, poultry, or shrimp. Savory and a little sweet, this dish is one of the first to go at get-togethers.

SERVES 4   PREPARATION TIME: 5 MINUTES + ½ HOUR SOAKING TIME   COOKING TIME: 6-8 MINUTES

1 lb (500 g) dried rice vermicelli noodles
2 tablespoons oil
8-12 cloves garlic, finely minced
3 large eggs
2 cups (400 g) very thinly sliced cabbage and carrots (coleslaw mix)
3 green onions (scallions), sliced into diagonals
2 tablespoons soy sauce
3½ tablespoons sweet soy sauce
¼ teaspoon salt
½ teaspoon ground white pepper
1 teaspoon paprika

1 Soak the rice vermicelli in warm water in a large bowl for ½ an hour to 1 hour until soft. Drain the vermicelli and set aside.

2 Heat the oil in a large wok over high heat; sauté the garlic until lightly browned and fragrant.

3 Crack the eggs into the wok and scramble until the eggs are nearly cooked. Add the cabbage and carrots and green onions, turning the heat down to medium high. Sauté thoroughly for just a minute until the cabbage and carrots begin to wilt.

4 Toss in the drained vermicelli, sauces, and dry spices. Sauté the vermicelli thoroughly for another 1 to 2 minutes. Serve as a vegetarian entrée or as a side dish to accompany a meat or poultry dish.

Stir-fried Noodles with Shrimp

Bakmie Goreng Udang

SERVES 4   PREPARATION TIME: 15-20 MINUTES
COOKING TIME: 10-15 MINUTES

12 oz (350 g) dried egg noodles or pasta
2 tablespoons oil
6-10 cloves garlic, finely minced
1 large shallot, finely minced
½ lb (250 g) fresh medium shrimp (about 12),
  shelled and deveined with tails left on
3 stalks Chinese broccoli (bok choy) rinsed and
  cut into 2 in long pieces
2 green onions (scallions), sliced
¾ teaspoon salt
½ tablespoon garlic powder
2 tablespoons sweet soy sauce
2 tablespoons Sriracha chili sauce (or any Asian
  chili sauce)
⅛ teaspoon ground white pepper

There are a few dishes available in every single restaurant across Indonesia that are universally loved and recognized as national dishes and Stir-fry Noodles with Shrimp is one of those dishes. For many of my childhood years, my family and I would order these noodles at every restaurant we frequented, whether at a stately hotel or a modest local one. Rich egg noodles are the alluring factor in this dish, gently stir-fried with thick, sweet soy sauce, and succulent shrimp. Pungent garlic, sweet shallots, and spicy Sriracha combine to lend an intoxicating scent of savory and spicy accents. Intensely green Chinese broccoli provides the added source of nutrients in this irresistible dish, though any leafy greens could be substituted. These stir-fried noodles are a delight for the palate and a kaleidoscope of vibrant colors for the eyes.

1 Bring a medium sized pot of water to a vigorous boil in a medium sized pot over high heat. Boil the noodles for 3 to 4 minutes then drain thoroughly. Set aside.

2 Heat the oil in a large wok over high heat, sauté the minced garlic and shallot in the oil for about 1 to 2 minutes until fragrant and translucent. Then add the shrimp and sauté them for another 1 to 2 minutes, until the shrimp are a bright pink-orange color on both sides.

3 Reduce the heat to medium and add the Chinese broccoli and green onion, stir-frying quickly.

4 Add the noodles, along with the salt, garlic powder, sweet soy sauce, chili sauce, and white pepper. Toss until the noodles, vegetables, and all the ingredients are thoroughly mixed, taking care to fold the noodles over with the spatula so as not to break them. Transfer to a large platter or bowl and serve hot.

SERVES 4
PREPARATION TIME: 5-10 MINUTES + ½ HOUR
SOAKING TIME
COOKING TIME: 12-15 MINUTES

8 oz (250 g) dried rice vermicelli noodles
2 tablespoons oil
6-8 cloves garlic, minced
4 cups (1 liter) water
4 cups (1 liter) chicken stock
12 oz (300 g) frozen or fresh meatballs (fish,
   beef, or pork)
1 teaspoon salt
2 teaspoons soy sauce
4 stalks mustard greens (or any leafy Asian
   greens), rinsed, sliced into lengths

GARNISHES
2 green onions (scallions), finely chopped
4 tablespoons Fried Garlic (page 27)
4 tablespoons Fried Shallots (page 34)
Sriracha chili sauce (optional)

1 Soak the rice noodles in warm water in a large
bowl for at least ½ an hour. Drain and set aside.
2 Heat the oil in a large pot over high heat and
sauté the garlic for 1 to 2 minutes until it turns
golden brown and fragrant. Pour in the water
and chicken stock and bring it to a vigorous boil.
3 Gently toss in the meatballs, salt, and soy
sauce. Simmer over medium high heat for 5
minutes before removing from the heat. Add
the mustard greens and stir thoroughly.
4 Divide the drained noodles evenly into 4
serving bowls. Ladle the very hot soup and
meatballs over the noodles. Garnish with
chopped green onions, Fried Garlic, and Fried
Shallots. Serve immediately.

Rice Noodle Soup with Meatballs
Bihun Kuah

My uncle and aunt used to own a small restaurant, where one of their specialties
was Rice Noodle Soup with Meatballs. Living in the United States during part of
my childhood, I only had the chance to visit my uncle, aunt and cousins during
summers and winter holidays. Eating at their restaurant was one of the best parts
of going home to Asia. Every time they knew that my family was coming, they'd
prepare the adults' table and kids' table. Smaller and shorter than the adults' table,
the kids' table would already be laden with piping hot bowls of Rice Noodle Soup
with Meatballs, overflowing with beef and pork meatballs, fried garlic, and green
onions (scallions). Soy sauce, sweet soy sauce, and all types of spicy chili sauces
sat nearby, waiting to turn the pristine white noodles into a bowl of hot lava. The
girls and I had competitions as to who could eat the spiciest soup and I always
won but not without having to take sips of cool, coconut water.

Noodle Soup with Spinach

Bakmie Kangkung

Noodle Soup with Spinach boasts a myriad of ingredients that, when combined, creates a sensual explosion of flavors. Rich egg noodles with a curly texture are the foundation of this recipe, layered underneath sweet, garlicky chicken morsels, and sautéed mushrooms. Fresh water spinach (*kangkung*) is a mellow flavored vegetable that adds an alluring swirl of vibrant greens (and healthy antioxidants). Noodle Soup with Spinach conjures one of the most humorous memories of my earlier years—finding my father, whom we thought was at an important meeting, at the local noodle shop by his office slurping on this wonderful soup after having postponed his supposedly crucial meeting. Yes, they are that good.

SERVES 4   PREPARATION TIME: 15-20 MINUTES
COOKING TIME: 15-20 MINUTES

1 lb (500 g) dried egg noodles
2 tablespoons oil
8-12 cloves garlic, minced
½ cup (125 g) diced white onion
2 pieces (1 lb/500 g) boneless, skinless chicken breasts, diced
1 tablespoon ground brown bean sauce
8 oz (250 g) straw mushrooms
1½ tablespoons soy sauce
½ tablespoon sweet soy sauce
Ground white pepper to taste
2 quarts (2 liters) chicken stock
½ lb (250 g) water spinach (*kangkung*), ends trimmed; or ½ lb (250 g) regular spinach rinsed and drained
½ teaspoon salt
3 green onions (scallions), rinsed and sliced
4 tablespoons Fried Garlic (page 27), to garnish

1 Bring the water to a vigorous boil in a large pot or wok over high heat. Add the dry egg noodles and gently stir around for 2 to 3 minutes. Use a fork to shake the noodles around as they begin to come apart. Drain the cooked noodles and divide equally into 4 serving bowls.
2 Heat the oil in a medium sized skillet or wok over high heat, sauté the garlic and onion until lightly browned and fragrant, for about 1 to 2 minutes.
3 Toss in the chicken and bean sauce, and stir-fry thoroughly for 4 to 5 minutes. Add the mushroom, soy sauce, sweet soy sauce, and white pepper. Continue to stir-fry for another 2 to 3 minutes. Spoon the ingredients over the noodles in the serving bowls.
4 Bring the stock to a vigorous boil in a large pot. Turn off the heat and gently place the water spinach in the stock along with the salt. Stir until thoroughly mixed. Ladle the soup over the noodles, sprinkle with green onions and serve immediately.

Savory Flat Rice Noodles

Kwee Tiauw

SERVES 4
PREPARATION TIME: 10 MINUTES + ½ HOUR SOAKING TIME
COOKING TIME: 13-15 MINUTES

1 lb (500 g) large, dried flat rice noodles (river noodles or hofun)
2 boneless, skinless chicken breasts
3 tablespoons oil
10-16 cloves garlic, minced
2 large shallots, minced
5 tablespoons thick black soy sauce
2 tablespoons soy sauce
3 tablespoons oyster sauce
¼ teaspoon ground white pepper
½ cup (125 ml) water
2 green onions (scallions), rinsed and sliced diagonally into 1 in (2.5 cm) lengths
1 cup (100 g) fresh bean sprouts

Indonesia's cuisine showcases a broad range of profound influences from neighboring cultures that, at some point in history, introduced different ingredients to the native chefs. Through the decades, this dish, featuring large, flat rice noodles, was never renamed from its original Chinese name. Kwee Tiauw has been adopted into mainstream Indonesian culinary language. I love the soft, thick texture of the flat, wide rice noodles, which beautifully absorb the various spices and sauces used in the recipe. Each bite yields the delicious taste of thick black soy sauce and oyster sauce.

1 Soak the rice noodles in warm water for at least ½ an hour. Drain and set aside.
2 Dice the chicken breasts and set aside.
3 Heat the oil in a large wok over high heat, add the garlic and shallots and sauté for 1 to 2 minutes until fragrant and lightly browned.
4 Toss in the chicken pieces and stir-fry for 2 to 2½ minutes.
5 Add the drained noodles to the wok. Stir-fry for about 3 minutes, taking care to fold the noodles over with the spatula so as not to break them. Reduce the heat to medium high.
6 Add the thick black soy sauce, soy sauce, oyster sauce, white pepper, and water. Toss the noodles to mix all the ingredients well. Add the green onion and bean sprouts. Toss again until well mixed and serve immediately.

Chapter Seven

Vegetables

If I had to choose one aspect of Indonesian cuisine that never fails to amaze me, it would have to be how vibrant and intense the flavors are in their vegetable dishes. These Indonesian dishes go beyond the typical or mundane stir-fries found in other cuisines. Hefty quantities of garlic along with a wide array of Indonesian herbs and spices (including shrimp paste and chili peppers) are used to flavor all types of vegetables, including nutritious eggplant and water spinach.

Pan-fried Tofu Omelet Tahu Telur

There are dishes from my childhood days that seemed so simple and I took them for granted whenever my mother made them. I thought I could always have Pan-fried Tofu Omelet whenever I felt like it, wherever I was—after all, it was just tofu and eggs. After moving out of my parents' house, I didn't get to eat this dish for years, not because it's difficult to prepare, but ironically because whenever the family was together, we would eat fancier, more complex dishes. I finally got my hands on my mother's recipe and now am able to satisfy my craving for this omelet with its sweet and savory sauce. This is really a classic Indonesian dish and is the perfect way to start the day, with something that tastes wonderful and gives a unique twist to a traditional breakfast favorite.

Pan-fried Tofu Omelet

SERVES 4
PREPARATION TIME: 5 MINUTES
COOKING TIME: 13-15 MINUTES

4 large eggs
¼ teaspoon salt
1 cake firm tofu (8 oz /250 g)
1 tablespoon oil
4 tablespoons parsley, roughly chopped

SAUCE
½ tablespoon oil
6 cloves garlic
½ tablespoon ground red chili pepper
½ tablespoon dried shrimp paste (Indonesian
   terasi or Thai shrimp paste)
2 tablespoons sweet soy sauce
½ tablespoon freshly squeezed lime juice

1 Whisk the eggs with the salt in a large bowl until well mixed and slightly frothy, 1 to 2 minutes, then set aside.
2 Drain the tofu and cut into small ½-inch cubes. Mix in with the whisked eggs and gently stir so the egg coats all the tofu cubes.
3 Make the Sauce by heating ½ tablespoon of oil in a small pan over medium high heat. Pan-fry the garlic and ground red chili pepper for about 1 minute until the chili pepper dries up. Allow for adequate ventilation, as frying chili pepper will cause tears and coughing.
4 Grind the fried garlic, and chili pepper with the shrimp paste using a mortar and pestle or food processor, until a smooth paste is formed. Transfer to a small bowl and pour in the sweet soy sauce and lime juice. Stir until thoroughly combined.
5 Heat a wok over medium high heat. After it's heated, add 1 tablespoon of oil. Carefully pour the tofu egg mixture into the wok. Using a spatula, gently push the cooked egg mixture towards the middle while slightly tipping the wok in a circular motion to keep the runny part of the eggs moving towards the outside. By doing this, you won't end up with a thick, uncooked portion in the middle. Make sure that the tofu cubes are evenly distributed throughout the omelet. Cook on one side for 4 to 5 minutes until slightly golden on the bottom. Then flip and cook for another 2 to 3 minutes on the other side. Gently slide the omelet onto a serving plate. Drizzle the Sauce over the tofu omelet and serve immediately.

Green Beans in Sweet Soy Tumis Kacang Panjang

With simple techniques, fresh ingredients, and aromatic herbs and spices, everyday vegetables take on a new character. Green Beans in Sweet Soy is as simple as it gets, with very little preparation and a short cooking time. Savory and nutritious on its own, it also serves as a wonderful side dish to meats or poultry. A little sweet, a little salty, and as much spice as you want to add, this Indonesian stir-fry lends intense flavors to crisp, fresh green beans.

1¼ lb (600 g) green beans, rinsed, trimmed,
   and sliced
½ tablespoon oil
1 tablespoon butter
7 cloves garlic, finely minced
1-2 bird's-eye chili peppers, sliced thinly on the
   diagonal (optional)
1½ tablespoons sweet soy sauce
1½ tablespoons regular soy sauce
1 tablespoon sambal oelek paste

SERVES 4
PREPARATION TIME: 10-15 MINUTES
COOKING TIME: 3-4 MINUTES

1 Heat the oil and butter in a wok over high heat. Once the butter has melted, toss in the garlic and, if using, the chili peppers. Sauté the garlic and peppers until lightly browned and fragrant.
2 Add the green beans, sweet soy sauce, soy sauce, and sambal oelek. Sauté for just about 1 minute until the green beans are crisp but tender. Serve on a bed of steamed white rice or as a side dish to meat or poultry dishes.

Spicy Potato Stir-fry — Sambal Goreng Kentang

Before the introduction of American fast food into Indonesia, there were no such things as French fries. Spicy Potato Stir-fry is Indonesia's own version of French fries, with a million times more flavor and far less guilt. Pan-roasting the potatoes gives them the golden crisp exterior everyone loves, while lots of garlic, chili peppers, and sweet soy sauce combine to create a savory glaze that makes mouths water as the first scent of the dish wafts through the air. Though Indonesians typically serve this as a side dish, I love eating it as a healthier snack alternative whenever I get a French fry craving.

SERVES 4 AS A SIDE DISH
PREPARATION TIME: 8-10 MINUTES
COOKING TIME: 13-15 MINUTES

6-8 cloves garlic, minced
1-2 bird's-eye chili peppers or ¼-½ teaspoon dried chili flakes
½ teaspoon sugar
2 tablespoons oil
3 potatoes, peeled and cubed (1½ lb/750 g)
2 tablespoons sweet soy sauce
½ teaspoon salt

1 Grind the garlic, chili peppers, and sugar into a smooth paste using a mortar and pestle or food processor.
2 Heat a wok over high heat. Add the oil and sauté the paste until fragrant for about 1 minute. Reduce the heat to medium high.
3 Carefully place the cubed potatoes in the wok and stir-fry for 8 to 12 minutes until the potatoes are golden and crisp on the outside.
4 Toss in the salt and sweet soy sauce, stir-frying for another minute until thoroughly mixed. Take care to fold the potatoes over when stir-frying instead of mashing them with the spatula. Serve as an accompaniment to a meat or poultry dish.

1 butternut squash (600 g)

6-10 cloves garlic

1 large shallot

2-3 bird's-eye chili peppers, finely chopped (optional)

½ tablespoon finely chopped galangal or ginger

1 tablespoon oil

2 stalks lemongrass, tender inner part of bottom
   third only, finely minced

1 teaspoon curry powder

1 cup (250 ml) coconut milk

2 tablespoons dark brown sugar or maple sugar (or
   Indonesian palm sugar)

1½ tablespoons tamarind concentrate or dried
   tamarind

3 star anise pods

¼ cup kaffir lime leaves, loosely packed and rinsed
   (20 leaves) or 2 teaspoons lime zest

1 teaspoon salt

1 teaspoon ground coriander

1 Peel the skin off of the squash. Slice the squash into bite-size chunks and set aside.

2 Grind the garlic, shallot, chili peppers, and galangal or ginger using a mortar and pestle or food processor, until they form a smooth paste.

3 Place a large pot or wok over high heat. Add the oil and sauté the paste along with the lemongrass and curry powder until fragrant, about 2 minutes.

4 Pour in the coconut milk and gently spoon in the squash. Stir thoroughly and allow the coconut milk to come to a vigorous boil. Then turn the heat down to medium high.

5 Add the dark brown sugar , tamarind, star anise pods, lime leaves, salt, and ground coriander to the stew. Stir until well mixed. Simmer for 20 to 30 minutes until the squash is fork tender. Serve with steamed white rice.

Butternut Squash Curry   Kare Labu

The squash and pumpkin family is very popular in certain regions of the Indonesia, with most dishes prepare them as either curries or desserts. Don't be intimidated by all the ingredients listed—they are all readily available at Asian grocery stores. If you can't find palm sugar (*gula jawa*) and tamarind cocentrate, you can substitute dark brown sugar and lime juice. Whenever possible though, try to use the original ingredients because any substitutions will inevitably alter the flavors. Combining creamy, spiced coconut milk with aromatic herbs, this dish is tender, savory, and sweet all at once. Butternut Squash Curry is a one-pot meal that is easy to prepare and keeps in the refrigerator for up to a few days.

Stir-fried Water Spinach with Shrimp Paste

Kangkung Cah Terasi

Kangkung is known as water spinach in the western hemisphere. It's not to be confused with watercress or potato leaves, although the latter appear deceptively similar. Water spinach is rich in anti-oxidant nutrients and essential fibers. This is one vegetable dish that even kids in Indonesia love to eat because of the sweet soy sauce and spicy chili. Be aware that stir-frying the shrimp paste may cause some people who are unaccustomed to Southeast Asian cuisine to run for their lives due to the unmistakably potent aroma.

SERVES 4   PREPARATION TIME: 10-15 MINUTES
COOKING TIME: 6-8 MINUTES

1 lb (500 g) water spinach (*kangkung*) or regular spinach
1½ tablespoons oil
6-10 cloves garlic, finely minced
1 large shallot, finely minced
2-3 bird's-eye chili peppers, minced
½ tablespoon dried shrimp paste (Indonesian *terasi* or Thai shrimp paste)
3 tablespoons sweet soy sauce
¼ teaspoon salt
½ cup (125 ml) water

1 Rinse the water spinach and drain thoroughly. Trim off any tough stems or wilted leaves. Cut the stems into 3-inch (8-cm) long pieces all the way to the leaves. Separate the stems from the leaves and set aside.
2 Heat a large wok over high heat. Add the oil and sauté the garlic, shallot, chili peppers, and shrimp paste for 1 to 2 minutes.
3 Place the water spinach stems into the wok first, stir-frying for a couple of minutes to soften the stems. Then add the rest of the water spinach and quickly stir-fry. Add the salt, sweet soy sauce, and water to the water spinach. Toss together thoroughly until all the sauces and spices are mixed well with the spinach. As soon as the leaves are wilted, the dish is ready. Serve immediately.

Sambal Eggplant Sambal Terong

The origins of this dish are unclear, but it probably is originally a Chinese or Sundanese dish. The Sundanese people live in the western half of the island of Java in Indonesia. This luscious eggplant dish is extremely popular in the capital city of Jakarta and surrounding areas. Eggplant has lots of nutrients and and when combined with shrimp paste chili, results in a dish packed with fiber. This is a great accompaniment to any main dish or even on its own as the main course, served on top of a bed of hot jasmine rice.

SERVES 4 AS A SIDE DISH
PREPARATION TIME: 5-7 MINUTES
COOKING TIME: 6-8 MINUTES

8 cloves garlic

1-2 bird's-eye chili peppers or 1-2 tablespoons sambal oelek

1 tablespoon dried shrimp paste (Indonesian *terasi* or Thai shrimp paste)

1½ lb (750 g) eggplant (2-3 large, long purple Asian eggplants or 1 globe eggplant)

3 tablespoons oil

½ cup (125 ml) water

3 tablespoons sweet soy sauce

1 Grind the garlic, chili peppers, and shrimp paste using a mortar and pestle or food processor, until it becomes a smooth paste. Set aside.

2 After trimming off the ends of the eggplant, slice it into bite-size chunks.

3 Heat a wok over medium high heat. Add the oil and sauté the dried shrimp paste mixture for 1 to 2 minutes until the kitchen (and probably the rest of the house) is filled with its unmistakably pungent aroma.

4 Toss in the eggplant and quickly stir-fry. Pour in the water and sweet soy sauce. Reduce the heat to medium high and continue to sauté for a few minutes until the eggplant is fork tender. Serve with steamed rice.

Chapter Eight

Desserts

A quick sampling of Indonesian desserts will immediately demonstrate that this nation is still very fond of homestyle cakes and confections made with natural ingredients rather than processed and overly sweet manufactured products. Most of the desserts in this chapter feature Indonesia's spectacular array of tropical fruits. Sweet Potatoes in Coconut Milk (page 109) with its exotic pandan leaves and palm sugar is perfect for cold days, while the national favorite, Tropical Shaved Ice with Fruit, is as visually stunning as it is flavorful and ideal for hot sultry days.

Dutch-Indo Crêpes with Palm Sugar Dadar Belanda

Several hundred years of Dutch occupation had profound effects on Indonesia's cuisine. However, in the years since independence, many foods whose roots are found in the colonial period are now thought to be purely Indonesian since the younger generations cook and eat them without realizing the impact of history on their cuisine. Dadar Belanda is similar to French crêpes dish although the condiments used are unique to Indonesia. This dessert is a source of fond memories as I recall sharing these crêpes with my parents and sisters at a mountain top resort in Indonesia called Puncak Pass. With the cold winds blowing and overlooking the lush tea bushes, we enjoyed these crêpes with a steaming cup of robust Javanese coffee.

MAKES 8 CREPES
PREPARATION TIME: 10 MINUTES
COOKING TIME: 12-15 MINUTES

5 large eggs (2 whole and 3 just the whites)
1 cup (250 ml) milk
⅛ teaspoon salt
¾ cup (150 g) all-purpose flour
1 teaspoon vanilla extract
½ tablespoon butter for the glaze + 4 tablespoons for the crêpes
3 tablespoons dark brown sugar or maple sugar (or Indonesian palm sugar)
1½ tablespoons water
Confectioners sugar for dusting

1 Whisk the eggs, milk, salt, flour, and vanilla in a large mixing bowl until smooth.
2 Heat a non-stick pan over medium high heat and melt ½ tablespoon of butter. Once the butter has melted, pour a medium sized ladle of the batter into the pan and quickly move the pan around to spread the batter evenly to form a thin coat. Cook on the first side for about 1 minute before using a flat spatula to flip over and cook for another 30 seconds. Both sides should be lightly golden. Repeat the above steps until the batter is gone.
3 Arrange the pancakes on serving plates.
4 In a small bowl, microwave the dark brown sugar and water for 45 seconds; stir until it has a smooth, syrup consistency. Alternatively, boil the Gula Jawa and water in a small pot, stirring until dissolved. Add ½ tablespoon of butter and mix thoroughly. Drizzle the syrup over the crepes and dust with confectioners sugar. Serve immediately.

Sweet Potatoes in Coconut Milk Kolak

Kolak has its roots in Eastern Java, where I spent several childhood years. I love this warm dessert on a cold evening or even as a snack in the afternoons. Tropical fruits and a sweet potato are gently boiled in coconut milk that is then sweetened with Javanese sugar (*gula jawa*). Also great when you're not feeling well from a cold or flu, this dessert is served warm and will satisfy your sweet tooth. It's difficult to find Indonesian restaurants overseas that serves this hearty dessert but you can make it at home and I'm sure you'll fall in love with it.

MAKES 1 MEDIUM SIZED POT
PREPARATION TIME: 15-20 MINUTES
COOKING TIME: 30 MINUTES

2 cups (500 ml) water
3 cups (750 ml) coconut milk
½ teaspoon salt
¾ cup (175 g) dark brown sugar or maple
    sugar (or Indonesian palm sugar)
Handful of pandanus leaves (or a few drops of
    pandanus essence or vanilla extract)
1 large sweet potato, cut into bite-size chunks
4 large ripe bananas, sliced into bite-size chunks
1 can (8 oz/250 g) jackfruit, drained and cut
    into thin slivers

1 Boil the water and coconut milk in a medium sized pot over high heat.
2 Once the coconut milk and water have come to a vigorous boil, lower the temperature to medium and simmer gently. Add the salt, dark brown sugar, and pandanus leaves and stir well.
3 Slide in the sweet potato chunks and simmer for 10 minutes until the potatoes are fork tender.
4 Add the bananas and jackfruit; simmer for another 10 minutes. Serve warm.

Banana Chiffon Cake Kue Pisang

Attending the Nila Chandra Culinary Academy when I was 12 years old was not easy. No one took me seriously, especially the teachers. On our first day, we learned how to make several desserts. (Nila Chandra was famous for her scrumptious desserts and was even in the Guinness Book of World Records for making the largest wedding cake at some point.) That same night at home, I decided it was time to prove to everyone that not only was I grown up enough to be in a cooking class with adults, but that I had more passion than any adult there. So I chose to bake a Banana Chiffon Cake and proudly brought it for my teachers to taste the next morning. They didn't believe that I had made it until my mother corroborated the fact that I had indeed baked it all by myself. Here is my version of this rich and moist Banana Chiffon Cake, that I've altered through the years to use ingredients available in Western markets.

MAKES 1 LARGE CAKE
PREPARATION TIME: 20-25 MINUTES
COOKING TIME: 45 MINUTES-1 HOUR

1¼ cups (300 g) unsalted butter at room temperature + for greasing
12 large eggs (12 yolks and 3 whites)
2 tablespoons condensed milk
1¾ cups (300 g) sugar
½ tablespoon pure vanilla extract
4 cups (500 g) all-purpose flour
1 teaspoon baking powder
½ teaspoon salt
3 ripe bananas, mashed

1 Preheat the oven to 350°F (175°C). Grease a 9-inch (20 cm) round baking pan with butter.
2 Beat or mix together the eggs, condensed milk, sugar, and vanilla in a bowl for 10 minutes on high speed until the batter rises and nearly doubles in volume.
3 Add the flour, baking powder, and salt, whisking for another 5 minutes.
4 Beat or mix the butter in a separate bowl until fluffy, then blend together with the mashed bananas until thoroughly combined.
5 Gently fold together the banana butter mixture with the egg batter until it is well mixed. Do not use an electric mixer for this step. Use a large spoon or spatula.
6 Pour the batter into the baking pan and bake for 45 minutes to 1 hour until a skewer inserted comes out just moist but not wet with batter. The exterior of the cake should be golden brown. Allow to cool for 15 minutes or so before cutting.

Banana Fritters Pisang Goreng

One of the most beloved foods in Indonesia, Banana Fritters are both a dessert and a snack for locals. This simple comfort food is so popular that it's sold everywhere in Indonesia, from five-star hotels to street stalls on dirt roads. If you ever have the chance to visit Indonesia and partake in the mad traffic on your way to some lovely destination, you can be sure that a young, hard-working child will run up to your car window attempting to sell you a couple of banana fritters. Through countless attempts, I've perfected this recipe that is one of the most popular with my own family and friends. It has a lightly crisp exterior and is soft and sweet on the inside.

MAKES 12 FRITTERS
PREPARATION TIME: 10-15 MINUTES
COOKING TIME: 10-15 MINUTES

Oil for deep-frying
6 large ripe bananas, peeled
1½ cups (175 g) self-rising flour
2 large eggs
½ teaspoon salt
½ teaspoon baking powder
½ cup (125 ml) coconut milk
½ cup (125 ml) club soda
Sweetened condensed milk for drizzling
 (optional)

1 Heat the oil in a large wok or fryer over medium high until the oil reaches 375°F (190°C). Alternatively, if you don't have a cooking thermometer, you can stick a chopstick in the oil and if bubbles appear then the oil is hot enough.
2 Cut the peeled bananas in half. Using the palm of your hand, gently press down on each of the banana halves to slightly flatten it. Set the bananas aside.
3 Mix together the flour, eggs, salt, baking powder, coconut milk, and club soda in a large mixing bowl until a smooth consistency is achieved.
4 Coat the bananas thoroughly in the batter and gently slip them one at a time into the hot oil. Fry a few bananas at a time and don't overcrowd them or they will stick together. Once a banana has turned golden brown on one side (after about 1 minute or so) gently flip it over and cook for about another minute until the other side is golden. Drain on paper towels and serve warm as is or drizzled with condensed milk.

Iced Sweet Young Coconuts

Es Kelapa Muda

A beautiful aspect of authentic, native Indonesian cuisine is the use of fresh produce and ingredients. Coconuts are a major commodity in Indonesia; in fact, this nation is arguably the world's largest producer of this popular fruit. Fresh young coconuts are quickly transformed into a refreshing, tropical dessert drink with a few added ingredients. Both rose and vanilla syrups can be found in Asian grocery stores and neither can be substituted. Serving this dessert right in its coconut shell is an incredible Indonesian delight, one that has become synonymous with the beautiful islands of this country.

SERVES 4
PREPARATION TIME: 20 MINUTES

4 young coconuts, husked and refrigerated
8 tablespoons rose syrup (not to be confused with rose essence; rose syrup is thick and red)
4 teaspoons vanilla syrup
Crushed ice for serving

1 Turn the coconut on its side. Using a heavy butcher knife, begin making cuts around the top of the coconut, about 2 inches from the center, in a circular pattern. This will result in a circular cut about 4 inches across. Do not cut through all the way as the coconut water will then spill out. You want to make cuts just deep enough so that when you stand the coconut upright, you can easily pry off the top with your hands, without losing any of the coconut water.
2 Once the top has been removed, set it aside and pour the coconut water into a large bowl.
3 Scrape the inside of the coconut with a spoon, using long, smooth strokes. Let the coconut flesh fall to the bottom of the coconut. Repeat steps 1 through 3 for all the coconuts.
4 Divide the syrups evenly between the coconuts.
5 Pour the coconut water back into the coconuts, making sure to leave a little room for the crushed ice. If there is any coconut water left over, save it in a separate glass for extra servings. Gently stir the coconut water and the syrups in each coconut until thoroughly mixed.
6 Carefully add to the crushed ice into each coconut. Place the tops back on and serve them on a plate with high edges or a large bowl to catch any spillage. Provide long spoons to scoop out the coconut flesh.

Iced Soursop Dessert Es Sirsak

It comes as no surprise that Indonesians have mastered the fine art of creating luscious desserts using a variety of fruits to combat the tropical heat. One of my favorites is this Iced Soursop, unforgettably fresh and tangy, and easy to make. In the West, *sirsak* is typically known as soursop or guanabana and may be difficult to find fresh. The frozen version is found in the freezer sections of most Asian grocery stores and even in some large western supermarkets along with other frozen fruits. It is also available in cans, but I don't recommend the canned version because the distinctive taste of the metal will ruin this light and fresh dessert. This dessert is fabulous on a hot day.

SERVES 4
PREPARATION TIME: 10 MINUTES

1¼ lb (700 g) frozen soursop pulp
2 cups (500 g) crushed ice
4-5 tablespoons sugar (adjust accordingly
    to the sweetness of soursop used as
    some may have added sugar already)
8 tablespoons evaporated milk for driz-
    zling

1 Defrost the soursop pulp until it is half frozen. Make sure to break any large frozen parts into smaller chunks.
2 Purée the soursop pulp using a blender or food processor with the crushed ice and sugar until smooth. Divide the mixture evenly into four serving glasses or bowls. Drizzle a few spoonfuls of evaporated milk over each glass and serve immediately.

Iced Coconut Cream with Jellies Es Cendol

There is something about the combination of coconut milk and palm sugar (*gula jawa*) that is just blissful. Iced Coconut Cream with Jellies is an addictive dessert that is often served as a snack or drink between meals. The chewy, slippery strips of green jelly add texture to create a dessert that perfectly complements a spicy meal. Though the green jellies do take some time to prepare, they can be made well in advance and stored in the refrigerator for up to 2 weeks.

SERVES 4
PREPARATION TIME: 25-35 MINUTES
COOKING TIME: 15-20 MINUTES

4 cups (1 liter) coconut milk

JAVANESE PALM SUGAR SYRUP
1 cup (250 ml) water
½ cup (175 g) dark brown sugar
    or maple sugar (or Indonesian
    palm sugar)

GREEN JELLIES
8 tablespoons tapioca flour
8 tablespoons rice flour
1 cup water (250 ml) (for the flour)
    + 2½ cups (625 ml) (for boiling)
4 pandanus leaves
Pinch of salt
Large bowl of ice water
2 cups (500 g) crushed ice

SPECIAL TOOL REQUIRED
A ladle with holes (Cendol strainer)

1 In a small pot, bring the coconut milk to a vigorous boil. Remove from the heat and set aside to cool.
2 Make the Javanese Palm Sugar Syrup by bringing the water to a boil, in another small pot, over high heat. Add the dark brown sugar and whisk until it is thoroughly dissolved. Remove from the heat and set aside to cool.
3 To make the Green Jellies, mix the tapioca and rice flours together in a medium sized bowl. Pour in 1 cup of water and continue to mix until thoroughly combined.
4 Bring a small pot of water to a boil over high heat. Drop in the pandanus leaves with the pinch of salt, stirring gently. Allow the pandanus leaves to boil for 5 minutes until the water turns green. If using pre-frozen pandan leaves, now add a few drops of green food coloring and stir until the color distributes evenly. Remove the pandanus leaves.
5 Lower the heat to medium. Pour the flour mixture into the boiling water. Using a whisk, quickly and continuously stir the mixture. It should begin to thicken immediately. Continue to whisk for about 4 to 6 minutes as the flour mixture cooks and thickens a little more. The color should turn from a powdery green to a more translucent green.
6 Remove the pot from the heat and set on a heat-safe plate or towel near the large bowl of ice water. Spoon a large dollop of the green jelly mixture into the cendol strainer and gently push it through with another spoon, allowing the long droplets to fall into the ice water. Repeat this step until all the green jelly mixture has been used. Make sure to gently stir the ice water every now and then so none of the droplets stick together.
7 Divide the Javanese Palm Sugar Syrup evenly between 4 serving glasses. Using the cendol strainer (or a ladle with holes), drain the Green Jellies and divide equally into the serving glasses on top of the syrup.
8 Add the crushed ice into each glass and top with the coconut milk. Serve immediately with long handled dessert spoons.

**Iced Coconut Cream
with Jellies**

Icy Sweet Melon Strips Es Blewah

Icy Sweet Melon and Rose Syrup is a lightly sweet, incredibly refreshing dessert beverage that brings together fresh melon and fragrant rose syrup. My mother made this simple but divine dessert throughout my childhood. It is so good that as a child, my older sister would run to the refrigerator to drink as much of it as she could when she knew that guests were coming. I guess some things are too good to share.

SERVES 6
PREPARATION TIME: 10-15 MINUTES
COOKING TIME: 0 MINUTES

1 small to medium-size ripe cantaloupe
4 cups (1 liter) ice-cold water
¾-1 cup (250 ml) rose syrup (not to be confused with rose essence; rose syrup is thick and red)
Crushed ice for serving

1 Cut the cantaloupe in half and remove the seeds.
2 Over a large mixing bowl, use the serrated end of a melon baller to scrape the flesh of the cantaloupe into long strips. It's very important to do this over the bowl to ensure that you catch as much of the juice as possible. A beautifully ripened melon will produce a lot of juice as you scrape out the flesh.
3 Add the ice-cold water and rose syrup. Stir thoroughly and serve on crushed ice in a tall serving glass or chill for a couple of hours and serve.

Iced Sweet Green Beans Es Kacang Hijau

Indonesia's tropical heat is one of the main reasons that desserts with cooling properties abound. Iced Sweet Green Beans is a local favorite on the streets of every city across Indonesia. Green mung beans are simmered until they reach a soft texture and impart a full-bodied flavor to the water. Sweetened with sugar and served over ice, this is a fresh, nutritious alternative to heavier cakes and sweets.

SERVES 4
PREPARATION TIME: 5 MINUTES + 2 HOURS OF SOAKING TIME
COOKING TIME: 50 MINUTES

1 cup (200 g) green mung beans
3 quarts (3 liters) water
1 cup (200 g) sugar
4 cups crushed ice

1 Soak the green mung beans in a bowl of cold water for at least 2 hours, up to overnight.
2 Drain the beans once they have soaked long enough. Bring 3 quarts (3 liters) of water to a vigorous boil in a pot. Stir in the drained green beans and lower the heat to medium high. Simmer for approximately 30 minutes, stirring occasionally.
3 Add the sugar, lowering the heat to medium and simmer for another 20 minutes until the beans begin to pop open. While simmering, continue to stir occasionally, making sure nothing sticks to the bottom of the pot.
4 Remove the pot from the heat and allow the beans to cool down for at least an hour in the sweetened water. When ready to serve, fill half of each serving glass with crushed ice. Then ladle the beans and sweetened water over the crushed ice and serve immediately. The beans can be kept in the refrigerator for up to 1 week.

SERVES 4
PREPARATION TIME: 15-20 MINUTES
COOKING TIME: 5 MINUTES

1 cup (250 ml) coconut milk
Pinch of salt
1 can (20 oz/565 g) lychee fruit, drained
1 can (20 oz/565 g) longan fruit, drained
1 ripe mango, pealed, pitted, and cubed
1 cup (250 g) strawberries, hulled and
   quartered
8 oz (250 g) coconut gelatin pieces (any
   color) or sweet jackfruit (fresh or canned)
6-8 cups ice cubes
½ cup (125 ml) sweetened condensed milk
½ cup (125 ml) rose syrup

1 Bring the coconut milk and pinch of salt to a boil in a small pot; set aside to cool.
2 Drain the syrup from the canned lychees and longans and place in a large bowl. Add the mango, strawberries, and coconut gelatin; mix together and set aside in the refrigerator for about 20 minutes.
3 Divide the fruit mixture evenly between four glasses.
4 Put ice cubes in a blender and crush them and layer over the fruit molding a mound on top.
5 Spoon the coconut milk over the ice equally. Drizzle the condensed milk and rose syrup over the ice (2 tablespoons for each glass). Serve immediately.

Tropical Shaved Ice with Fruit
Es Campur

This is a version of a traditional Indonesian dessert called *Es Campur*, which literally translates into "Mixed Ice." Tropical Shaved Ice with Fruit is a refreshing dessert to top off any meal or to have as a cold treat on a hot afternoon. The combination of sweet and sour fresh fruits against a mellow backdrop of coconut milk infused with a drizzle of creamy condensed milk and exotic rose syrup. Rose syrup, an essential ingredient for this dessert, can be found in your local Asian grocery store and is widely available online. The rose syrup's fragrant scent and unique flavor make this addictive dessert distinctive and memorable.

Index

Acknowledgments

This book is dedicated to my father, mother and grandfather, who collectively taught me about love, family and food.

Heartfelt gratitude towards everyone who has impacted my life in immeasurably positive ways, but in particular those who helped bring this book to fruition:

Neil Salkind, for believing in me, giving me the first chance and continuing to patiently mentor me.

My sisters for being lifelong recipe guinea pigs and constant laughter.

Giovanni for his relentless love, dedication and putting up with the constant madness.

Rachane for his patient love and for the funny arguments over which way the knife should sit.

Jenny for her years of friendship and sisterly support.

Johan and Hamilton for their profound friendship and sharing countless dinners "around the world."

Chef Glenn Chu of Indigo Hawaii, Chef Greg Cole of Celadon Napa and Letty Alvarez of LA Sweets for their friendship and kind support.

The Living Greens team for opening their kitchen to me.

Olga and Noe Flores for their tireless support and genuine caring.

William Notte and Eric Oey at Tuttle for seeing my potential.

Bud Sperry, for his editing expertise, patient guidance and supportive friendship.

And many thanks to my generous allies—Zojirushi Rice Cookers and Lee Kum Kee.

Published by Tuttle Publishing, an imprint of Periplus Editions (HK) Ltd.

www.tuttlepublishing.com

Yuen, Dina.
  Indonesian cooking : a culinary journey across Indonesia, from bali
to java and beyond / Dina Yuen ; foreword by Glenn Chu.
    p. cm.
  Includes index.
  ISBN 978-0-8048-4145-0 (hardcover)
1. Cooking, Indonesian. I. Title.
  TX724.5.I5.Y84 2012
  641.59598--dc23

                              2011022510

ISBN 9780804841450

Distributed by
North America, Latin America & Europe
Tuttle Publishing
364 Innovation Drive, North Clarendon, VT 05759-9436 U.S.A.
Tel: 1 (802) 773-8930; Fax: 1 (802) 773-6993
info@tuttlepublishing.com; www.tuttlepublishing.com

Japan
Tuttle Publishing,Yaekari Building, 3rd Floor,
5-4-12 Osaki, Shinagawa-ku, Tokyo 141-0032
Tel: (81) 3 5437-0171; Fax: (81) 3 5437-0755
sales@tuttle.co.jp; www.tuttle.co.jp

Asia Pacific
Berkeley Books Pte. Ltd, 61 Tai Seng Avenue, #02-12, Singapore 534167
Tel: (65) 6280-1330, Fax: (65) 6280-6290
inquiries@periplus.com.sg; www.periplus.com

Printed in Hong Kong   1110EP
15 14 13 12   6 5 4 3 2 1

TUTTLE PUBLISHING® is a registered trademark of Tuttle Publishing,
a division of Periplus Editions (HK) Ltd.

The Tuttle Story
"Books to Span the East and West"

Most people are very surprised to learn that the world's
largest publisher of books on Asia had its beginnings in the
tiny American state of Vermont. The company's founder,
Charles E. Tuttle, belonged to a New England family
steeped in publishing. And his first love was naturally
books—especially old and rare editions.

Immediately after
WW II, serving in
Tokyo under General
Douglas MacArthur,
Tuttle was tasked with
reviving the Japanese
publishing industry,
and founded the
Charles E. Tuttle Publishing Company, which still thrives
today as one of the world's leading independent publishers.

Though a westerner, Charles was hugely instrumental in
bringing knowledge of Japan and Asia to a world hungry
for information about the East. By the time of his death
in 1993, Tuttle had published over 6,000 titles on Asian
culture, history and art—a legacy honored by the Japanese
emperor with the "Order of the Sacred Treasure," the
highest tribute Japan can bestow upon a non-Japanese.

With a backlist of 1,500 books, Tuttle Publishing is as
active today as at any time in its past—inspired by Charles'
core mission to publish fine books to span the East and
West and provide a greater understanding of each.

About the Author

Hailing from a mixed Chinese and Russian background, Dina Yuen spent her childhood years between Indonesia, Singapore, and the United States. She was blessed with a family who possessed a strong sense of tradition and love for food. From the early age of 5, she already found a profound passion for cooking, lavishing her family with new creations constantly. To her parents' great shock, Dina demanded to go to cooking school while in Indonesia.

After receiving her parents' approval, she still had to convince the founder of the culinary school that a 12-year-old child was capable of keeping up with her adult peers. Persistence and dedication paid off as Dina became the youngest student to ever graduate from the Nila Chandra Culinary Academy. After studying the intricacies of Asian and European techniques and flavors, she went on to travel the world with her family. For the next ten years, she studied with numerous chefs of both top hotels and local hole-in-the-wall restaurants. In Indonesia specifically, Dina's knowledge of the local cuisine deepened through further studies with chefs at the Dharmawangsa Hotel, Sheraton Bali, Amandari Bali, Nyonya Tanzil, and Sultan Hotel (formerly the Hilton Jakarta).

Though she fulfilled her parents' wishes of graduating in Industrial Engineering and Business Management, Dina decided to forge a different path in the past several years. After catering numerous friends' parties and hosting many of her own, she founded *Asian-Fusion.com*, an all in one portal that showcases the best of Asia through cuisine, travel, art, music, and much more. Through Asian Fusion, she has also become a well connected and respected food and travel critic, forming close relationships with many notable chefs, corporations and hotels including Lee Kum Kee, Chef Glenn Chu of Indigo, Chef Jay Mariadoss formerly of Taj Hotels, the Ritz Carlton, and Aman Resorts.

Indonesian Cooking is Dina's debut cookbook where she shares both her own recipes as well as those passed down from her mother and grandmother. With articles published in various Asian and women's magazines, Dina has recently completed her historical novel *The Shanghai Legacy*, and is also working on her second cookbook, *A Tour of Thailand* as well as her debut non-fiction book, *Top 25 Women Leaders of the 21st Century*.

In the near future, she plans to open a chain of Asian cafés in the United States before expanding in Asia.

http://www.theasianfusiongirl.com
http://www.asian-fusion.com